GRANDMA USED TO BAKE . . .

. . . better-tasting food from better-tasting ingredients—like whole grains and honey.

All the oldies and goodies are included here—from porridges to shortbreads, breakfast foods and coffee cakes, griddle cakes and waffles, donuts and fritters, side dishes like mushes and fried breads, and wonderful cookies of all kinds.

Take it from the author, and prove it with your own palate:

The modern cook can't go astray
cooking the whole grains and honey way!

WHOLE GRAINS
AND HONEY

EUGENE KOWALSKI

PYRAMID BOOKS • NEW YORK

WHOLE GRAINS AND HONEY

A PYRAMID BOOK

First printing, February 1973

ISBN 0-515-02957-2

Printed in the United States of America

Pyramid Books are published by Pyramid Communications, Inc. Its trademarks, consisting of the word "pyramid" and the portrayal of a pyramid, are registered in the United States Patent Office.

PYRAMID COMMUNICATIONS, INC.
919 Third Avenue
New York, New York 10022, U.S.A.

CONTENTS

FOREWORD

The past few years have seen a rising concern throughout our rich nation about the emptiness of much of the food we eat. Our search for the good life has led us, inadvertently, to give up much of the good of life . . . many of the good things that nature provides for our delight.

It is not our contention that we should do as grandmother did. Convenience foods are indeed convenient, and none of us would want to do without most of them. But we do object to losing the good that nature provides . . . not only the nutritional good, but most particularly the food flavors we've lost without really meaning to.

This book, therefore, is written for the modern cook and homemaker who wants to enjoy food more. It is based on two simple facts—that most of today's recipes started with yesterday's products, and that grandmother's food tasted better not because she worked harder to make it so, but because the ingredients she used—ingredients which are still readily available today—had more flavor.

After trying the recipes in this book, the inventive homemaker will undoubtedly find many more ways to use the delicious flavors of whole grains and honey to delight her family.

—EUGENE KOWALSKI

ABOUT INGREDIENTS

The flours called for in the following recipes are whole-grain flours. Wheat flour means graham, whole-wheat, or entire wheat. Rye means rye meal, dark or light rye flour, or pumpernickel flour. The variety of names indicate whether the bran has been removed or left in, and the names vary with locations.

For cornmeal, try to find some made from the entire corn kernel. Rice means brown rice. Rolled oats are rolled oats, but you'll probably prefer to buy them from a miller, a health-foods store, or a store that specializes in grains.

We've called for "shortening" throughout, to encourage you to use your favorite—*except* in the recipes that depend on a specific shortening for their characteristic flavor (cookies, for instance). Even in these, you're naturally free to substitute your favorite—just be aware that it alters the flavor slightly. Where sugar is called for, raw sugar is equally good and brown sugar can be used, but it will change the flavor.

The whole-grain flours are available in health-foods stores and special shops in most large cities. They're available nationwide direct-by-mail from several millers whose ads appear in the mail-order sections of nutrition, foods, and women's magazines.

CHAPTER I

MUSHES AND PORRIDGES

INTRODUCTION

It can't be said too often that breakfast is the most important meal of the day. The morning meal sets the tone for the entire day, and if you skimp on it, it affects you ... whether you feel it at the moment or not.

Breakfast should be high in protein for lasting energy, with a good supply of carbohydrates for quick energy to start you out right. It should be appealing to the taste, filling at the moment, and lasting.

A bowl of hot cereal with milk and honey or sugar meets all of these requirements. As the foundation of a breakfast, combined with meat, fruit or juice, bread if you like, hot cereal helps you start the day with the feeling of well-being you need for any kind of activity.

Oatmeal is by far the most common and popular breakfast cereal, with the other commonly packaged cereals ... farina, etc. ... running a close second. But there are many others to try, different, delicious and nutritious, with flavors that should please your family and add variety to the most important meal of the day.

COOKING AND SERVING

Cereals must be cooked in boiling liquid before they are edible. They are done when they start to thicken, which takes more or less time depending on the consistency of the cereal and the liquid used to cook it.

Most of the following recipes call for water in the cooking. Milk can be substituted for the water in equal measure, and you may wish to use milk, as well as adding milk to the cereal, if you are cooking for children. You can also use fruit juice, in which case, the cereal won't thicken quite as much.

Coarse cereals should be dropped into boiling water slowly, so the grains have time to soak up the water individually, instead of sticking to each other. Fine cereals like cornmeal should be mixed with a little cold water, to start the moisturizing process, before you add them to the boiling liquid.

Serve cereal in an attractive shallow bowl ... a porringer, if you have one, or a soup or dessert bowl. Sprinkle with sugar, or pour on honey or molasses to taste. Most children—and many adults—prefer cereal with cold milk as well as sweetening. Others, particularly adults, relish a chunk of butter melted in the warm cereal. Either way, it's a hearty, attractive dish on the breakfast table.

RECIPES

RECIPE #1

CORNMEAL MUSH

1 cup cornmeal	*1 teaspoon salt*
1 cup cold water	*4 cups boiling water*

Mix the cornmeal and salt with the cold water. Gradually add to the boiling water in the top of a double boiler, stirring continually. Cover and let simmer, stirring occasionally. It will be ready to eat in about 15 minutes, but can be cooked longer if convenient. Just keep stirring it from time to time.

4 generous servings

RECIPE #2

FRIED MUSH

Fried cornmeal mush is classic, but many of the following recipes can also be used this way. Cook the mush until it's rather thick (not as thin as you'd normally use for cereal). Put it in flat baking tins and refrigerate until it's cold and solidified (or refrigerate the cereal left from breakfast, and serve it as fried mush the next day).

TO COOK: Cut the cold mush into squares and fry in any hot shortening until golden brown and warmed through. Serve with breakfast meat, with honey or molasses or syrup or jam poured over the mush.

RECIPE #3

OATMEAL

This is the long-cooking steel-cut oats. For rolled oats, simply follow the directions on the package.

2 cups oatmeal   4 cups boiling water
1 teaspoon salt

Sprinkle the oats in the boiling salted water (have the top part of the double boiler on the burner to start the cooking). Cook for four or five minutes, then set over the lower boiler, cover, and cook for about three hours, stirring occasionally.

VARIATIONS: Add ½ cup raisins, or ½ cup diced cooking apples for the last 15 to 20 minutes.

4 generous servings

RECIPE #4

GRAHAM PORRIDGE

1 cup graham flour   1 teaspoon salt
1 cup cold water   4 cups boiling water

Mix the flour, salt and water into a smooth paste. Stir the mixture into 4 cups of boiling water in the top of a double boiler. Cook for 20 minutes, stirring occasionally.

VARIATION: Add ½ cup chopped dates for the last few minutes of cooking.

4 generous servings

RECIPE #5

BUCKWHEAT PORRIDGE

1 cup buckwheat flour *1 teaspoon salt*
1 cup cold water *4 cups boiling water*

Follow directions for cornmeal mush, RECIPE #1. Leftover buckwheat porridge makes very good fried mush.

4 generous servings

RECIPE #6

RYE PORRIDGE

1 cup rye flour *1 teaspoon salt*
1 cup cold water *4 cups boiling water*

Follow directions for Graham Porridge, RECIPE #4. This is very tasty served with molasses and butter.

4 generous servings

RECIPE #7

CRACKED WHEAT PORRIDGE

1 cup cracked wheat *3 cups boiling water*
1 teaspoon salt

Sprinkle the cracked wheat into the salted boiling water in the top of a double boiler. Cover and cook for about 3 hours, stirring occasionally.

4 generous servings

RECIPE #8

WHEAT GERM PORRIDGE

½ cup wheat germ
½ teaspoon salt

1½ cups boiling water

Sprinkle the wheat germ into the salted boiling water in the top of a double boiler. Cover and cook for an hour, stirring occasionally.

4 servings

RECIPE #9

HASTY PUDDING

2 cups cold milk
2 cups cornmeal
2 teaspoons wheat flour

1 teaspoon salt
4 cups boiling water

Stir the cornmeal and flour into the cold milk. Gradually stir into the boiling salted water in the top of a double boiler. Boil for 30 minutes, stirring occasionally. This is good used for fried mush.

4 to 6 servings

RECIPE #10

MILLET PORRIDGE

1 cup shelled millet seed	*1 teaspoon salt* *3 cups water*

Bring all ingredients to a boil and boil for 1 minute. Cover and simmer for 15 to 20 minutes, or until soft.

4 generous servings

RECIPE #11

HONEYED RICE

1 cup rice *1 tablespoon sugar* *1 tablespoon butter*	*2 cups milk* *2 tablespoons honey*

Bring the milk, sugar and butter to the boiling point and sprinkle in the rice, stirring continually. Let the mixture boil again, stir once more, cover and turn the heat very low. Let the rice simmer for 25 minutes without uncovering. Stir in the honey and serve hot.

4 generous servings

RECIPE #12

HONEYED BARLEY

¾ cup barley
½ teaspoon salt
3 cups boiling water

2 tablespoons butter
3 tablespoons honey

Sprinkle the barley into the boiling salted water and simmer for 1½ hours, or until tender. Pour off any excess water, add the butter to the hot barley, and cover until the butter melts. Stir in the honey and serve.

4 to 6 generous servings

CHAPTER II

BREAKFAST BREADS AND COFFEE CAKES

INTRODUCTION

The recipes in this chapter are for the light, sweet breads that are so popular with coffee or tea for breakfast or a midmorning snack. Made with whole grains, they are more nutritious than usual—and tastier, too.

Of course, the not-so-sweet recipes for Quick Breads, Muffins and Biscuits (Chapter VI), and some of the yeast breads and rolls (Chapter V) are also welcome on the breakfast table, and some of these breakfast breads go well with a dinner that needs a sweet side dish.

COOKING AND SERVING

These breads are quite light, and rise with baking powder or baking soda. They should be mixed thoroughly but lightly (beating too well may make them heavy). They're best when served warm from the oven with butter or margarine.

RECIPES

RECIPE #1
QUICK CAKE

½ cup shortening
½ cup sugar
2 eggs
½ cup milk

1½ teaspoons baking
  powder
½ teaspoon salt
2 cups wheat flour

Cream butter and sugar. Beat in eggs and milk. Add flour, salt and baking powder and mix thoroughly but lightly. Bake in well-greased 9″ square pan at 350° for about 20 minutes. Sprinkle with powdered sugar and serve.

RECIPE #2

QUICK COFFEE CAKE

1½ cups wheat flour
1½ teaspoons baking
   powder
½ teaspoon salt

½ cup brown sugar
¼ cup shortening
1 egg
½ cup milk

TOPPING:

2 tablespoons
   shortening
4 tablespoons brown
   sugar

1 tablespoon wheat
   flour
2 teaspoons cinnamon

Rub the shortening into the flour. Stir in the baking powder, salt and sugar. Beat the egg into the milk, then mix into the dry ingredients lightly but thoroughly. Pour into a well-greased 9" square pan. Rub together all the ingredients for the topping, and sprinkle it over the cake. Bake at 350° for about 20 minutes.

RECIPE #3

RAISIN CAKE

½ cup shortening
½ cup sugar
½ cup molasses
1 tablespoon lemon juice
2 eggs

½ cup milk
2 cups wheat flour
½ teaspoon soda
1 cup raisins

Cream the butter and sugar. Beat in the molasses and lemon juice. Add the well beaten eggs and milk, then stir in the flour and soda lightly but thoroughly. Stir in raisins, pour into well-greased 9" x 13" pan, and bake at 350° for 20 to 25 minutes.

RECIPE #4

MIXED GRAIN QUICK BREAD

1 egg
½ cup molasses
1 cup buttermilk
½ cup melted
  shortening
1 cup wheat flour
½ cup rye flour

½ cup cornmeal
½ teaspoon soda
1 teaspoon baking
  powder
1 teaspoon salt
½ cup raisins

Beat the egg, and mix in the molasses, buttermilk, and melted shortening. Add the flours, cornmeal, soda, baking powder, and salt, and mix lightly but thoroughly. Stir in the raisins and bake in a well-greased bread pan for about 45 minutes. Let cool for 10 minutes in the pan, then turn out the loaf, cool for 10 minutes more, slice and serve warm with butter or margarine.

RECIPE #5

BREAKFAST BISCUITS

3 cups wheat flour
1 teaspoon baking
  powder
½ teaspoon soda

½ teaspoon salt
¼ cup sugar
2 eggs
about 1 cup milk

Mix the flour, baking powder, soda, salt and sugar, Beat the eggs well and mix with ½ cup milk. Add to the dry ingredients, and mix in enough more milk to make a light, workable dough. Roll out and cut into biscuit shapes, or shape with your hands into 2-inch cakes. Bake at 425° for about 15 minutes. Serve with butter and honey.

18 or 20 2-inch biscuits

RECIPE #6

CINNAMON BUNS

½ cup shortening
2 cups wheat flour
1 teaspoon baking
  powder

¼ teaspoon salt
about ⅔ cup milk
soft butter
sugar and cinnamon

Rub the butter into the flour; add salt and baking powder, then mix in enough milk to make a fairly stiff, workable dough. Roll out into a large thin sheet. Spread well with soft butter, sprinkle liberally with sugar and cinnamon, roll up and slice into buns. Bake at 350° for about 20 minutes.

12-15 2-inch buns

RECIPE #7

SWEET WHEAT BREAD

1 egg
½ cup molasses
¼ cup brown sugar
¼ cup melted
  shortening
1 teaspoon grated lemon
  rind

1½ cups wheat flour
½ teaspoon cinnamon
¼ teaspoon salt
1 teaspoon soda
⅔ cup yogurt

Beat the egg; add molasses, sugar, melted shortening and lemon rind. In a separate bowl, mix the flour, cinnamon, salt and soda. Add the egg mixture and the yogurt to the dry ingredients, and mix lightly but thoroughly. Bake in a well-greased bread pan at 425° for about an hour. Cook in pan for 10 minutes, turn out of pan and cool about 10 minutes more, then slice and serve warm with butter.

RECIPE #8

QUICK BRAN BREAD

1 egg	1 teaspoon baking
¾ cup buttermilk	powder
¼ cup molasses	½ teaspoon salt
1 cup bran	½ teaspoon soda
1 cup wheat flour	½ cup raisins or nuts
	(optional)

Beat the egg with the buttermilk and molasses. Beat in the bran, flour, baking powder, salt and soda. Stir in raisins or nuts, if you like. Bake in well-greased bread pan at 375° for about an hour. Cook in pan for 10 minutes, turn out and cool for 10 minutes more, then slice and serve warm with butter.

RECIPE #9

SOUR CREAM COFFEE CAKE

1 cup sour cream	2 teaspoons baking
2 eggs	powder
1½ cups wheat flour	½ teaspoon soda
1 cup sugar	¼ teaspoon salt

TOPPING:

2 tablespoons	1 tablespoon wheat
shortening	flour
4 tablespoons brown	2 teaspoons cinnamon
sugar	

Beat the eggs well and blend well with the sour cream. Add the flour, sugar, baking powder, salt and soda. Beat lightly until well mixed. Pour into a well-greased 9″ square pan. Rub together all the ingredients for the topping, and sprinkle over the coffee cake. Bake at 350° for about 20 minutes.

RECIPE #10

HONEY-WHEAT COFFEE CAKE

2 cups wheat flour	½ teaspoon salt
¾ cup sugar	½ cup shortening
2 teaspoons baking powder	1 egg plus 1 egg yolk
	about ¾ cup milk

TOPPING:

½ cup sugar	¼ cup honey
¼ cup shortening	½ cup crushed nuts
1 egg white	½ teaspoon cardamon

Rub the shortening into the flour, and mix in the sugar, baking powder and salt. Break one egg into a measuring cup, add an egg yolk (reserving the white for the topping) and fill the cup with milk. Beat well and add to dry ingredients. Pour into greased 9″ x 13″ pan. Cream sugar and shortening for topping. Blend in unbeaten egg white. Add honey, nuts, cardamon, mix well and spread on coffee cake. Bake at 350° for about 25 minutes.

CHAPTER III

GRIDDLE CAKES AND WAFFLES

INTRODUCTION

Whether they're called griddle cakes, pancakes or flapjacks, these light, smooth, tasty cakes are an American favorite. Nearly every family has its favorite recipe, often a weekend special that father cooks and serves with pride.

Waffles, too, are apt to be a family specialty, with a traditional recipe or a traditional filling that makes them a real breakfast treat.

Made with whole grains, these breakfast favorites are more nutritious, and much more flavorful.

Here are some different and interesting ways to make both griddle cakes and waffles with a variety of whole grains and a wide variety of flavorings. Any one of them is apt to become a new favorite with *your* family.

COOKING AND SERVING: GRIDDLE CAKES

Griddle cake batter should be rather thin and mixed very lightly, with no attempt to get out all the lumps. It can be made several hours in advance, and held in a covered dish in the refrigerator.

A well-seasoned griddle or skillet is best for cooking griddle cakes, because it should need no greasing. The griddle is ready when a few drops of cold water bounce and sputter on it. If the cakes stick on the pan you're using, rub it lightly with shortening as needed.

To make nicely shaped round cakes, pour the batter from the tip of a spoon onto the center of the griddle. Cook the first side until bubbles form on the top, then turn with a spatula and cook the second side about half as long as the first. If your first cake is thicker than you like, thin the batter with a little more liquid; if too thin, add a little flour.

Griddle cakes should be served hot as soon as they're cooked; if necessary, you can hold them in a slow oven for a few minutes, but they do get soggy very quickly.

Most people like griddle cakes with butter or margarine and syrup, honey, jam, jelly, etc. For especially nourishing breakfast, sandwich a couple of strips of bacon or sausage patty between two griddle cakes, and top the stack with an egg or two.

RECIPES

RECIPE #1

WHEAT CAKES

1½ cups wheat flour
2 tablespoons brown
  sugar
½ teaspoon salt
½ teaspoon baking
  powder

¾ teaspoon soda
1 egg
2 cups milk
4 tablespoons melted
  shortening

Mix together the flour, sugar, salt, baking powder and soda. Beat the egg into the milk, add the melted shortening and mix the liquid into the dry ingredients very lightly

12 to 14 cakes

RECIPE #2

BUTTERMILK WHEAT CAKES

1 cup wheat flour
1 teaspoon baking
  powder
½ teaspoon soda
¾ teaspoon salt

1 egg
1 cup buttermilk
2 tablespoons honey
4 tablespoons melted
  shortening

Mix together the flour, baking powder, soda and salt. Beat the egg, then combine it with the buttermilk, honey and melted shortening. Mix the liquid into the dry ingredients very lightly.

VARIATION: For the 1 cup of wheat flour, substitute ⅓ cup each wheat flour, rye flour and cornmeal.

About 8 to 10 cakes

RECIPE #3

BUCKWHEAT CAKES

1 cup buckwheat flour
1 teaspoon baking
    powder
½ teaspoon salt
1 egg

1 cup milk
2 tablespoons molasses
2 tablespoons melted
    shortening

Mix together the flour, baking powder and salt. Beat the egg, then combine it with the milk, molasses and melted shortening. Mix the liquid into the dry ingredients very lightly.

About 12 cakes

RECIPE #4

ONION BUCKWHEAT CAKES

1 cup buckwheat flour
½ cup cornmeal
1 teaspoon baking
    powder
1 teaspoon soda
1 tablespoon brown
    sugar
1 egg

1½ cups milk
½ cup sour cream
2 tablespoons melted
    shortening
1 cup finely chopped
    onion
2½ tablespoons
    shortening

Mix together the flour, cornmeal, salt, baking powder, soda and sugar. Beat the egg into the milk, blend in the sour cream and melted shortening, and stir the liquid into the dry ingredients very lightly. Saute the onions in the remaining shortening until translucent and tender, then fold into the batter.

VARIATION: Substitute rye flour for the breakfast flour.

About 20 cakes

RECIPE #5

BATTER CAKES

2 eggs
2 cups cornmeal mush
½ teaspoon salt

2 tablespoons honey
½ cup wheat flour
about 2 cups milk

Beat the eggs and mix them with the cornmeal mush. Beat in the salt, honey and flour. Add enough milk to make a fairly thin batter.

15 to 18 cakes

RECIPE #6

CORNMEAL GRIDDLE CAKES

2 cups cornmeal
1 teaspoon salt
2 tablespoons honey
1 cup boiling water
2 eggs

1 cup milk
4 tablespoons melted
butter
2 tablespoons wheat
flour

Put the cornmeal, salt and honey in a bowl, pour the boiling water over them, cover and let stand for 10 minutes. Beat the eggs into the milk. Combine the melted butter and flour, beat into the milk mixture, and stir lightly into the cornmeal mixture.

VARIATION: Fold 1 cup finely chopped cooking apples into the batter.

15 to 18 cakes

RECIPE #7

RICE GRIDDLE CAKES

1 cup boiled rice   *2 tablespoons flour*
½ cup milk   *½ teaspoon salt*
3 eggs

Separate the eggs. Beat the yolks into the milk, then combine with the rice, flour and salt. Beat the egg whites until stiff and fold into the rice mixture. Cook at once on a *greased* griddle or skillet. (Note: Since these cakes have no shortening in the batter, they require grease on the cooking surface.)

8 to 10 cakes

RECIPE #8

RICE CORNMEAL GRIDDLE CAKES

½ cup wheat flour   *1 cup rice boiled*
1 teaspoon salt   *2 eggs*
½ teaspoon soda   *2 cups buttermilk*
1 tablespoon sugar   *2 tablespoons melted*
½ cup cornmeal   *shortening*

Mix together the flour, salt, soda, sugar and cornmeal. Add the rice. Separate the eggs. Beat the yolks into the buttermilk, add the shortening, and mix the liquid into the dry ingredients. Beat the egg whites until stiff and fold into the rest of the batter lightly. Cook immediately.

About 12 cakes

RECIPE #9

OATMEAL GRIDDLE CAKES

½ cup wheat flour
1 teaspoon baking
  powder
½ teaspoon salt
1 egg

1½ cups cooked
  oatmeal
¾ cup light cream
2 tablespoons melted
  shortening

Mix together the flour, baking powder and salt. Beat the egg into the cream, mix with the oatmeal and shortening, and stir the mixture into the dry ingredients very lightly.

About 12 cakes

RECIPE #10

EGG-RICH TINY PANCAKES

4 eggs
½ cup wheat flour

½ cup milk
¼ teaspoon salt

Beat the eggs well, add the flour, salt, and about half the milk and beat until smooth. Gradually add the rest of the milk, beating continually, until you have a batter the consistency of heavy cream. Allow about a tablespoon of batter for each pancake; cook on lightly greased skillet.

VARIATION: Add 1 tablespoon vanilla sugar and 1½ teaspoons grated lemon rind to the batter.

About 16 tiny pancakes

RECIPE #11

VERY RICH BUCKWHEAT PANCAKES

1 cup buckwheat flour
2 tablespoons sugar
3 eggs
1 cup light cream

2 tablespoons sherry
¼ teaspoon grated
  nutmeg

Mix the flour and sugar together. Beat the eggs into the cream. Add the sherry and nutmeg, and mix the liquid into the dry ingredients very lightly. Cook on lightly greased skillet. Serve sprinkled with powdered sugar and fresh lemon juice.

About 10 cakes

RECIPE #12

FESTIVE FLAPJACKS

These are perfect for late holiday breakfasts or brunches.

¾ cup wheat flour
¼ teaspoon salt
2 eggs
1 cup milk

4 tablespoons honey
2 tablespoons brandy
vanilla sugar

Mix the flour and salt together, beat the eggs into the milk, and combine the liquid and dry ingredients lightly. Cook small cakes on a lightly greased skillet. Mix the honey and brandy together. While the flapjacks are warm, spread them with the honey mixture, roll them up, sprinkle with vanilla sugar and serve.

COOKING AND SERVING: WAFFLES

These dainty cakes are as easy to prepare as they are delicious. To make them perfectly light, they should be cooked immediately after the stiffly beaten egg white is folded into the rest of the batter. Cover about ⅔ of the waffle iron with batter, close it, and wait until it's stopped steaming. If it's hard to open, leave it for another minute.

Although they're traditionally served for breakfast with honey or jelly or syrup, waffles are also excellent for lunch or dinner with creamed meat or cheese. And they make a superb dessert topped with fruit and ice cream or whipped cream.

RECIPES

RECIPE #13

WHEAT WAFFLES

1½ cups wheat flour
½ teaspoon salt
2 teaspoons baking
    powder
2 tablespoons brown
    sugar

2 eggs
1¼ cups milk
5 tablespoons melted
    shortening

Mix together the flour, salt, baking powder and sugar. Separate the eggs. Beat the yolks into the milk, add the melted shortening and mix the liquid into the dry ingredients very lightly. Beat the egg whites until stiff and fold into the rest of the batter.

VARIATIONS: For the 1½ cups wheat flour, substitute ½ cup each wheat flour, rye flour, cornmeal. Substitute molasses for the brown sugar.

4 or 5 waffles

RECIPE #14

CORNMEAL WAFFLES

1½ cups cornmeal	3 eggs
½ cup wheat flour	1½ cups buttermilk
2 teaspoons baking powder	3 tablespoons honey
½ teaspoon salt	½ cup melted shortening

Mix together the cornmeal, flour, baking powder and salt. Separate the eggs. Beat the yolks, add to the buttermilk and mix in the honey and melted shortening. Mix the liquid into the dry ingredients very lightly. Beat the egg whites until stiff and fold into the rest of the batter.

About 6 waffles

RECIPE #15

BACON CORNMEAL WAFFLES

Prepare batter for Cornmeal Waffles, RECIPE #14, using 4 tablespoons melted shortening instead of ½ cup. Cut thin slices of bacon into quarters. As you pour the waffles, put a piece of bacon on each quarter of the waffle iron. It will cook right into the waffle.

About 6 waffles

RECIPE #16

RICE WAFFLES

1½ cups wheat flour
1 teaspoon baking
    powder
½ teaspoon salt
½ cup boiled rice

2 eggs
1¼ cups milk
4 tablespoons melted
    shortening

Mix together the flour, baking powder and salt. Add the rice. Separate the eggs. Beat the yolks into the milk, add the melted shortening, and combine the liquid with the dry ingredients very lightly. Beat the egg whites until stiff and fold into the rest of the batter.

About 6 waffles

RECIPE #17

RICE AND CORNMEAL WAFFLES

½ cup wheat flour
½ cup cornmeal
½ teaspoon baking
    powder
1 teaspoon salt

1 cup boiled rice
2 eggs
1½ cups milk
4 tablespoons melted
    butter

Mix together the flour, cornmeal, baking powder, and salt. Add the rice. Separate the eggs, and beat the yolks with the milk. Add the melted shortening, and mix the liquid with the dry ingredients very lightly. Beat the egg whites until stiff, and fold lightly into the rest of the batter.

About 6 waffles

RECIPE #18

DARK GINGERBREAD WAFFLES

These are very good for dessert, served with a custard sauce, whipped cream or ice cream.

½ teaspoon instant coffee

⅓ cup firmly packed brown sugar

½ cup dark molasses

1 cup boiling water

1 cup wheat flour

1¼ teaspoons soda

1 teaspoon ground ginger

¼ teaspoon ground clove

1 teaspoon ground cinnamon

½ teaspoon salt

1 egg

Combine the instant coffee, sugar, and molasses with the boiling water and let cool. Mix together the flour, soda, spices and salt. Beat the egg well, add it to the cooled liquid, and mix the liquid lightly with the dry ingredients.

VARIATION: Substitute rye flour for the wheat flour.

4 thin waffles

CHAPTER IV

DOUGHNUTS AND FRITTERS

COOKING AND SERVING: DOUGHNUTS AND FRIED BREADS

Doughnuts are made from a dough thick enough to roll out, and cut with a doughnut cutter in the traditional hole-in-the-middle shape. The hole serves two purposes—letting the fat circulate and cook the entire doughnut evenly, and permitting the dough to expand on all sides, which gives it a light, delicate grain.

Raised doughnuts are made with yeast and must be allowed to rise before they're cooked. *Cake or plain doughnuts* are made with baking powder or soda, and absorb less of the cooking grease if they're allowed to stand in the open air and dry for about 10 minutes before they're cooked.

Cook doughnuts in enough fat to cover them, in a heavy skillet or kettle or a deep fryer. The fat should be at 375° on a fat thermometer—or you can test it by dropping in a small piece of the dough you're going to use. If it pops right up to the top, and cooks to a crisp, non-greasy golden brown in about a minute, your fat is ready to use.

Each doughnut takes about 3 minutes. Cook the first side until it's brown enough, then turn the doughnut and do the other side. If you turn it frequently, it absorbs more grease.

Let the cooked doughnuts drain on absorbent paper until they're cooled a little, then sprinkle with plain, powdered or cinnamon sugar and serve while warm. They will keep for a few days, and are good cold or warmed in the oven. For a breakfast treat, slice a cold doughnut in half, toast it in the toaster, and serve with butter.

The fried breads are cooked the same as doughnuts. Any variations are explained in the recipes that follow. Drain them well when cooked, and serve in a napkin-lined basket while warm.

RECIPES

RECIPE #1

PLAIN DOUGHNUTS

2 cups wheat flour
1 teaspoon salt
2 teaspoons baking
  powder

4 tablespoons sugar
1 cup milk

Mix everything together, chill dough for about 20 minutes, and roll out or pat about ½ inch thick. Cut with a doughnut cutter, let shapes rest for about 10 minutes, and slide each doughnut into hot fat with a spatula. Cook for about 3 minutes, until both sides are golden brown. Drain, sprinkle with plain, powdered or cinnamon sugar, and serve.

12 to 15 doughnuts

RECIPE #2

SPICE DOUGHNUTS

2 cups wheat flour (or
  1 cup each wheat and
  buckwheat flour)
2 teaspoons baking
  powder
½ teaspoon cinnamon
½ teaspoon salt
¼ teaspoon cloves

¼ teaspoon nutmeg
¼ teaspoon ginger
1 egg
½ cup sugar
2 tablespoons melted
  shortening
½ cup milk

Mix together the flour, baking powder, salt and spices. Beat the egg well, then beat in the sugar until thoroughly mixed. Add the shortening and milk, mix the liquid with the dry ingredients thoroughly, chill, and proceed as in Recipe #1 above.

VARIATION: Add ½ cup nuts or raisins

12 to 15 doughnuts

RECIPE #3

SOUR CREAM DOUGHNUTS

4 cups wheat flour	1 teaspoon nutmeg
1 teaspoon soda	½ teaspoon cinnamon
2 teaspoons baking powder	1 cup sugar
½ teaspoon salt	3 eggs
	1 cup sour cream

Mix together the flour, soda, baking powder, salt, and spices. Beat the eggs, beat in the sugar, add the sour cream, and stir the liquid into the dry ingredients thoroughly. Chill and proceed as in Recipe #1.

VARIATION: Add ½ cup chopped dates

About 25 doughnuts

RECIPE #4

RAISED DOUGHNUTS

1 package (or cake) yeast	½ teaspoon cinnamon
1¼ cup warm water	½ teaspoon salt
½ cup shortening	1 cup sugar
4 cups flour	2 eggs

Sprinkle the yeast over ¼ cup of the warm water, sprinkle on a little sugar, and set it aside. Rub the shortening into the flour, mix in the cinnamon, salt, and sugar. Beat the eggs, add to the rest of the warm water, and mix the liquid into the dry ingredients. Add the yeast, which should be active and foamy, and mix everything well. Set the mixture in a warm place and let rise until about double in bulk (about 2 hours). Punch down and knead lightly on floured board, then roll out to about ½ inch thick. Let the dough rest until it starts to rise again, then cut into doughnut shapes and let rise for another 15 minutes or so. Slide each doughnut with a spatula into hot fat and fry until golden brown.

About 25 doughnuts

RECIPE #5

JELLY DOUGHNUTS

Prepare dough for Recipe #4, Raised Doughnuts but save about a tablespoon of egg white. Roll out to ¼ inch thick instead of ½ inch. Cut into rounds instead of doughnut shapes. On half of the round put a teaspoonful of jelly, preserves, etc. Brush the edges of the dough with egg white, and top each with another round, pressing the edges together firmly. Let rise for about 15 minutes, and fry.

About 20 doughnuts

RECIPE #6

CHOCOLATE DOUGHNUTS

4 cups wheat flour
1 teaspoon soda
2 teaspoons baking
   powder
½ teaspoon salt
1¼ cups sugar

2 tablespoons
   shortening
4 ounces (squares)
   baking chocolate
3 eggs
1 cup milk
1½ teaspoons vanilla

Mix together the flour, soda, baking powder, salt and sugar. Melt the shortening and baking chocolate together, and cool. Beat the eggs, beat in the cooled chocolate and shortening, and mix with the milk and vanilla. Stir the liquid into the dry ingredients thoroughly, chill, and proceed as in Recipe #1.

About 25 doughnuts

RECIPE #7

MOLASSES DOUGHNUTS

2 cups wheat flour
2 cups rye flour
2 teaspoons baking
   powder
1 teaspoon soda
2 teaspoons ginger

½ teaspoon salt
½ cup sugar
2 eggs
¾ cup molasses
1 cup sour cream

Mix together the flours, baking powder, soda, ginger, salt and sugar. Beat the eggs and beat them into the molasses. Mix with the sour cream and mix the liquid with the dry ingredients thoroughly. Chill, and proceed as in Recipe #1.

RECIPE #8

WHEAT CRULLERS

3 cups wheat flour
1 teaspoon baking
    powder
½ teaspoon soda
½ teaspoon salt
½ cup brown sugar

4 eggs
½ teaspoon grated
    lemon rind
4 tablespoons melted
    shortening
¼ cup milk

Mix together the flour, baking powder, soda, salt and sugar. Beat the eggs until quite light, then add the lemon rind, shortening and milk. Mix the liquid into the dry ingredients thoroughly. Chill, roll out about ¼ inch thick, and cut into about 3-inch strips. Twist a couple of times and fry.

RECIPE #9

RAISED RICE CRULLERS

½ package (cake) yeast
½ cup lukewarm water
¾ cup boiled rice
3 eggs

⅓ cup sugar
½ teaspoon salt
¼ cup wheat flour
¼ teaspoon nutmeg

Sprinkle the yeast on the water, and sprinkle on a little sugar. Mash the rice. When the yeast is light and fluffy, mix it with the rice. Cover the bowl and let it stand overnight at room temperature. In the morning, beat the eggs well and add them and all the other ingredients to the rice mixture. Mix well and drop from a teaspoon and deep fry until golden brown. Drain well and serve sprinkled with powdered sugar.

RECIPE #10

PLAIN DROP DOUGHNUTS

3½ cups wheat flour
1 cup sugar
1 teaspoon salt
½ teaspoon nutmeg

2 teaspoons baking
    powder
3 eggs
1 cup milk

Mix together the flour, sugar, salt, nutmeg and baking powder. Beat the eggs well and mix them with the milk. Stir the liquid into the dry ingredients thoroughly. Drop from a spoon, deep fry until golden brown, and drain well.

About 40 doughnuts

RECIPE #11

JOLLY BOYS (CORNMEAL DROP DOUGHNUTS)

2 cups cornmeal
1 cup boiling water
½ cup sugar
½ teaspoon salt

½ teaspoon soda
1 cup wheat flour
1 egg

Pour the boiling water on the cornmeal, beating well. Let stand for 10 to 15 minutes. Mix the sugar, salt, and soda with the flour. Beat the egg well and beat into the cooled cornmeal mixture. Add the dry ingredients and mix thoroughly. Drop from a spoon and deep fry until golden brown.

About 24 doughnuts

RECIPE #12

HONEY FRIED BREAD

This is a special treat for your family while they're waiting for your fresh bread to come out of the oven.

Save a piece of any bread dough, roll it out half an inch thick, cut into strips about 4-inches long, and deep fry for a couple of minutes until they're golden brown. Drain and serve with butter, and hot honey.

RECIPE #13

SOPAIPILLAS

1½ cups wheat flour
2 teaspoons baking
  powder
¾ teaspoon salt

2 tablespoons
  shortening
½ cup lukewarm water

Mix together the flour, baking powder and salt, and rub in the shortening. Pour in the water and work the dough with your hands until you can gather it into a ball (if too dry, add a few more drops of water). Knead the dough on a lightly floured surface for about 5 minutes, until smooth and somewhat elastic. Let rest for 15 minutes. Roll out into a large circle and cut into wedge-shaped pieces; or roll out into a large rectangle and cut into squares. Deep-fry, turning frequently, until light, puffy, and golden brown. Drain and serve with butter and honey.

8 wedge-shaped pieces, or 12 squares

RECIPE #14

NAVAJO FRY BREAD

2 cups wheat flour
2 teaspoons baking
  powder
½ teaspoon salt

2 tablespoons
  shortening
½ cup ice cold milk

Mix together the flour, baking powder and salt, and rub in the shortening. Pour in the milk and work the dough with your hands until you can gather it into a ball. Cover with a towel and let rest at room temperature for about 2 hours. Divide the dough into 3 pieces, and roll out each piece into an 8-inch round. Make two parallel slits in each piece—about 4 inches long and 1 inch apart, in the center of the round. Deep fry for about 2 minutes on each side until slightly puffy, crisp and brown.

3 8-inch rounds

RECIPE #15

COLLEGE PUDDINGS

An excellent deep-fried dessert that uses up left-over bread

2 cups bread crumbs (wheat, oatmeal or cornmeal bread is best)
¾ cup melted shortening
½ cup raisins or currants

½ cup nuts or ¼ cup chopped peel or fruit-cake mix
⅓ cup sugar
½ teaspoon nutmeg
3 eggs
4 tablespoons brandy (or ½ teaspoon brandy flavoring)

Put the bread crumbs into a mixing bowl, pour on the melted shortening and mix together well. Add the raisins, nuts, sugar and nutmeg and mix together. Beat the egg well, add the brandy, and beat into the bread crumb mixture until well mixed. Shape into balls and deep fry, turning each piece 2 or 3 times until golden brown. Drain well and serve with powdered sugar, hard sauce or wine or lemon sauce.

About 20

RECIPE #16

FRIED BISCUIT DESSERT

2 cups wheat flour
4 teaspoons baking
  powder
1 teaspoon salt
4 tablespoons
  shortening

1 egg
about ½ cup milk
jam, jelly
egg white

Mix together the flour, baking powder and salt and
rub in the shortening. Beat the egg, (holding out a
little of the white, and work into the flour lightly.
Add enough milk to make a fairly firm dough, and
knead lightly on lightly floured board. Roll out
about ⅛" thick and cut into large rounds (3" or 4"
diameter). Put a spoonful of jam, jelly, etc. in the
center of each round, brush the edges of the dough
with the egg white, fold over and press together.
Deep fry for 2 or 3 minutes, until golden brown.
Drain and serve, sprinkle with powdered sugar if
you like.

COOKING AND SERVING: FRITTERS

Fritters are trully versatile, useful foods—a great way to use up almost anything leftover—a superb addition to any meal. Try fruit fritters as a breakfast bread, a dinner bread, a dessert—vegetable fritters as a side dish for lunch or dinner—meat fritters as the main course at lunch, or a breakfast dish. The variety is endless.

A fritter is almost anything wrapped or dipped in batter and deep fried (and the word is also used for light doughnut-type deep-fried breads with fruit or vegetables mixed in). The secret to perfect fritters is to make the batter the right consistency for the food you're wrapping or dipping—for instance, juicy fruits need a firmer batter than dry meats. The recipes in this chapter can be varied in endless ways with an endless variety of foods—just use your imagination a little and you can make a fritter out of almost any kind of cooked meat or vegetable as well as fruits.

Fritter batter is improved by letting it rest for a couple of hours before frying, or even overnight in the refrigerator. The following recipes call for adding the stiffly beaten egg whites just before using the batter. This is not essential. You can use whole eggs instead of separated eggs when you first mix up the batter—but it does make lighter, puffier fritters.

Deep fry fritters for 3 or 4 minutes at 375°. Be sure to drain them well before serving.

RECIPE #1

PLAIN ALL-PURPOSE FRITTER BATTER

1½ cups wheat flour   *about 1¼ cup milk*
½ cup cornmeal   *1 teaspoon salt*
2 eggs

Mix together the flour, cornmeal and salt. Separate the eggs, beat the yolks well, mix with half the flour and beat the liquid into the dry ingredients. Add enough more milk, beating well, to make a batter the consistency you'll need—thinner if you're dipping fruit or vegetable pieces in it, thicker if you're mixing in berries or bits of meat or vegetable. Cover and refrigerate for a few hours, or overnight. Beat the egg whites until stiff and fold into the batter just before you use it. Dip in slices of fruit like apples, banana, etc; or pieces of cooked meat, slices of vegetables like eggplant, yellow squash, etc. into the batter or stir in berries, nuts, bits of chopped meat or cooked chopped vegetables. Drop by spoonfuls into deep fat, fry, drain and serve.

VARIATIONS: For fruit, add 1 tablespoon sugar; and/or substitute juice from the fruit for part of the milk. For meat or vegetables, beat a tablespoon of vinegar or lemon juice into the mixture before adding the last of the milk.

RECIPE #2

SPICY BEER BATTER FOR MEAT OR VEGETABLE FRITTERS

*1½ cup wheat or
buckwheat flour*
1 teaspoon salt
*¼ teaspoon pepper
(black or cayenne)*

*1 tablespoon melted
shortening or olive oil*
2 eggs
about ¾ cup flat beer

Mix together the flour, salt, pepper and shortening. Separate the eggs, beat the yolks well, and beat into the flour mixture. Add the beer slowly, beating continually, until the batter is the consistency you want. Cover and refrigerate for a few hours or overnight. Beat the egg whites until stiff, and fold into the batter just before using it. Proceed as in Recipe #1.

VARIATION: Add ½ teaspoon of any herb seasoning that you like with the meat or vegetable you're cooking—thyme, sage, basil, tarragon, etc. (But don't season the batter if the meat is already seasoned!)

RECIPE #3

WINE BATTER FOR FRUIT FRITTERS

1 cup cornmeal	1 egg
½ cup wheat flour	about 1 cup wine (sweet
2 tablespoons sugar	or dry, but not sharp
½ teaspoon salt	or sour)

Mix together the cornmeal, flour, sugar and salt. Separate the egg, beat the yolk well, mix it with half the wine and beat into the dry ingredients. Add enough more wine to make a batter the consistency you want. Cover and refrigerate for a few hours or overnight. Beat the egg white until stiff and fold into the batter just before using it. Proceed as in Recipe #1.

VARIATION: Add to the batter any sweet spice you like—1 teaspoon cinnamon, ½ teaspoon nutmeg or ginger, ¼ teaspoon clove, etc. Add ½ teaspoon grated lemon rind or 1½ teaspoons lemon juice if you're using very sweet wine or very sweet fruit.

RECIPE #4

APPLE FRITTERS (BASIC FRUIT FRITTERS)

Make Recipe #1 or Recipe #3, thin enough to dip in the fruit. Choose rather large, well-shaped cooking apples. Pare and core them, and slice them crosswise into rings about ¼-inch thick. Sprinkle the rings with sugar (and lemon juice, if you like) and let stand for about an hour. Dip the rings in batter and deep-fry. Sprinkle with sugar before serving.

Bananas, fresh or canned peaches, fresh pears and most other firm fruits can also be prepared this way.

RECIPE #5

BANANA FRITTERS

1 cup wheat flour
½ cup cornmeal
½ teaspoon salt
3 eggs

6 tablespoons honey
1 cup milk
about 1 pound ripe
   bananas

Mix together the flour, cornmeal and salt. Beat the eggs, beat in the honey, and mix in half of the milk. Beat the liquid into the dry ingredients, then add milk, beating constantly, until you have a batter that will pour from a spoon smoothly and slowly. Mash the bananas to a thin puree, then stir them in the batter and let it rest at room temperature for about 30 minutes. Drop from a spoon, about ¼ cup at a time, into hot fat, and deep fry for about 3 minutes. Drain, sprinkle with powdered sugar and serve warm.

RECIPE #6

RUM-LIME BANANA FRITTERS

*Recipe #1, thin enough
  for dripping fruit*
¼ cup light rum
1 tablespoon strained
  fresh lime juice

2 tablespoons sugar
3 medium-size bananas,
  ripe

Make Recipe #1, adding 2 tablespoons sugar. Combine the rum, lime juice and sugar in a mixing bowl and stir well until the sugar is dissolved. Peel the bananas, cut them crosswise into 1-inch slices; and drop them into the rum mixture, tossing lightly to coat them well. Let them marinate for about an hour, turning them occasionally. Drain and dry the banana slices, dip them in the batter and deep-fry for 3 or 4 minutes. Drain and serve.

VARIATION: Use ¼ Brandy in the marinade, in place of the rum and lime juice.

RECIPE #7

CORNMEAL FRITTERS

4 eggs
3 cups milk
2 cups cornmeal
1 tablespoon sugar
1 tablespoon melted
  shortening

1 teaspoon salt
½ cup flour
½ teaspoon baking
  powder

Separate the eggs, beat the yolks well; and stir in the milk, cornmeal, sugar, melted shortening and salt. Mix together the flour and baking powder and beat into the cornmeal mixture. Beat the egg whites until stiff and fold them into the batter. Drop by spoonfuls into hot fat, fry for 3 or 4 minutes, and drain well. Serve for breakfast with a sauce made of butter, sugar and cinnamon; or with butter as a side dish for lunch or dinner.

VARIATION: Add to the batter 1 cup fresh or well-drained canned corn kernels (these can also be mixed into Recipe #1 or Recipe #2).

RECIPE #8
CURRANT FRITTERS

1 cup milk	3 tablespoons boiled
2 tablespoons wheat	rice
flour	3 tablespoons currants
4 eggs	¼ cup sugar
	¼ teaspoon nutmeg

Beat the flour into the milk. Beat the eggs well, and mix them and the rest of the ingredients into the batter. Drop by spoonfuls into hot fat, fry until golden brown, drain and sprinkle with powdered sugar. Serve with lemon wedges.

RECIPE #9
INDIAN FRITTERS

3 tablespoons wheat	2 eggs
flour	2 more egg yolks
boiling water	

Put the flour in a mixing bowl and beat in enough boiling water, a few tablespoons to make a stiff paste, beating well to keep the mixture smooth. Cool, and beat in 2 whole eggs and 2 more egg yolks. Drop by spoonfuls into deep fat and fry until golden brown. They should puff up nicely. Serve with jam or marmalade as a bread with lunch or dinner; or with syrup or honey for breakfast.

RECIPE #10

BERRY FRITTERS

2 eggs	½ teaspoon cinnamon
½ cup milk	2 cups fresh strawber-
½ cup heavy cream	ries, raspberries, blue-
1 tablespoon cornstarch	berries, blackberries,
4 tablespoons sugar	raisins, nuts, etc.

Beat the eggs, add the milk and cream, and thicken with the cornstarch. Beat in the sugar and cinnamon, and fold in the fruit. Deep-fry by spoonfuls, drain, and serve with powdered sugar; or stir the fruit in Recipe #1 or Recipe #3.

RECIPE #11

ORANGE FRITTERS

Make Recipe #1 or Recipe #3. Choose oranges that are easy to peel and separate. Peel them as thoroughly as possible and separate them into sections without breaking the skin (unless the seeds are close to the surface and easy to remove). Dip in the batter and deep fry until golden brown; drain and serve sprinkled heavily with powdered sugar.

VARIATION: Instead of separating oranges, slice them paper thin. You can prepare lemons this way, too.

RECIPE #12

PINEAPPLE FRITTERS

Recipe #3
1 small pineapple

¼ cup brandy or liqueur
¼ cup powdered sugar

Make Recipe #3 substituting heavy cream for the wine. Peel and core the pineapple, and slice into thin rings. Mix the brandy and powdered sugar in a bowl, and soak the pineapple slices in the mixture for at least 4 hours. Drain them and dip in the batter; deep-fry for 6 or 7 minutes, drain, and serve sprinkled with powdered sugar.

RECIPE #13

RICE FRITTERS

1 cup boiled rice
2 eggs
1 tablespoon wheat flour

½ teaspoon salt
1 teaspoon cinnamon

Beat the eggs and stir them into the rice, then stir in the flour, salt and cinnamon and mix thoroughly. Deep-fry by spoonfuls until brown.

VARIATION: Substitute ¼ cup marmalade for the cinnamon.

CHAPTER V

YEAST BREADS

INTRODUCTION

Naturally, the flavorful whole-grain flours really come into their own when baked into tasty loaves of rich-flavored homemade bread.

If you're not a regular bread-baker, the first thing you should know about baking bread is that it's *easy*. The procedure is so simple it's almost foolproof . . . and it really doesn't take a lot of your active time. You do have to be on hand for a few hours to tend the dough when it needs it, but it probably won't take an hour of handling altogether.

The only equipment you need is a very large, heavy bowl—the kind grandmother had. A soup kettle or large pan will do, but a bowl is nicer and easier to work with.

This chapter includes several basic recipes using various kinds of flour. As you get acquainted with the way the different flours behave, you'll mix them freely and come up with new and delicious combinations.

One fine ingredient for almost any kind of bread is almost any kind of leftover breakfast cereal.

Simply add it to the dough (no more than a cup for an ordinary two-loaf recipe).

There's something very satisfying about providing your family with bread you bake yourself. If you haven't tried it yet, you'll certainly enjoy the feeling of accomplishment . . . and the praise of family and friends . . . the first time you do.

BASIC INSTRUCTIONS

All raised bread doughs need flour, liquid, yeast . . . and all also call for some kind of flavoring (salt, sugar, sometimes a little spice) and usually shortening. Bread rises because the yeast, encouraged to grow by liquid at the proper temperature, acts on the gluten in the flour to form gas bubbles that give the bread its light texture. Wheat flour has more gluten than any other flour, and most breads call for at least part wheat flour. The exception is rye bread. This can be made with all rye flour, which has some gluten in it, but it will never be quite as light as wheat bread.

The first step in baking bread is starting the yeast. Follow the instructions on the package . . . sprinkle dry yeast (or crumble a yeast cake) over a little warm water, and set it aside for a few minutes while it starts working. It will start faster if you sprinkle a little sugar over it.

The usual liquid for bread is milk, which contributes the moist, cake-like texture of good bread. (Water is used in light, dry French or Italian breads.) Scald the milk, then cool it to lukewarm— the yeast dies when exposed to high temperatures, and you want it alive and active until time to bake the bread. When the milk is cool enough, stir in about a cup of flour to form a thin paste, and add a little salt, sugar and shortening and any other flavoring called for. Then add the yeast and mix it in well. If you like, let this mixture rest until the yeast starts to cause bubbles . . . this step isn't essential, but it will let you know the yeast is working properly, and it starts you toward a nice, smooth dough.

Next, stir in the rest of the flour, to make a dough thick enough to be handled. Bread dough must be kneaded to break down the gluten in the flour. This is what makes even, smooth-textured bread. The less gluten in the dough, the longer you should knead it—about 5 minutes for plain wheat bread, up to 10 minutes for rye or other heavy doughs. Depending on the recipe, you knead the bread before it rises the first time—or after it rises the last time. When you're through kneading, the dough should be smooth, feel resilient as you press it, and almost stop sticking to your hands and the board.

Dough can rise once, twice, or several times, depending on the kind of flour you're using and the results you're after. Cover the dough with a clean cloth and set it in a warm (not hot) place, out of drafts, while it rises. The rule of thumb is to let it about double in bulk each time it rises. More than that doesn't help the texture, but simply permits big gas bubbles to form.

The last rising is in the bread pan. Shape the dough into loaves by turning and patting it in your hands, tucking in the sides and ends until you have a fairly even, rectangular loaf. Press it into the well-greased pan and cover it with a clean cloth. It should fill the pan about two-thirds when you put it in, and it's ready to bake when it's risen just enough so it begins to clear the top of the pan.

Bread is done when it's golden brown and crusty and sounds hollow when you tap the top or bottom with your finger.

RECIPE #1

PLAIN WHEAT BREAD

This is a very light wheat bread—much lighter than most. The trick is in letting it rise several times.

1 package (or cake) yeast	1/4 cup shortening
1/4 cup lukewarm water	2 teaspoons salt
2 cups milk, scalded	About 6 cups wheat flour
1/4 cup honey	

Sprinkle the yeast on the water (follow the directions on the package). You can sprinkle a little sugar on it to make it work faster. Put the honey and shortening into a large bowl and pour the scalded milk over them to melt them. Stir well. When the mixture has cooled to lukewarm, stir in the salt, the yeast, and two or three cups of flour. Beat well until very smooth, then add more flour, a little at a time, until the dough is too stiff to beat with a spoon. Mix it well, cover, and let rise until double in bulk. Punch the dough down, turn it over in the bowl, and let it rise again. Repeat twice more (until the dough has risen (four times). When you've punched it down the fourth time, turn it out on a floured board and knead it for at least 10 minutes, keeping the board dusted with flour as needed. Shape the dough into two loaves, put it into well-greased bread pans, and let it rise until it just clears the top of the pans. Bake at 450° for 15 minutes (you must have the oven pre-heated), then lower the oven temperature to

350° and bake for another 30 minutes or so, until done.

VARIATIONS: Add 1 cup raisins or 1 cup chopped onion, sauteed until transparent, or 1 cup chopped cooking apples and a teaspoon cinnamon.

RECIPE #2

MIXED GRAIN MOLASSES BREAD

This has a chewy, pumpernickel-like texture and an interesting flavor.

*1 package (or cake)
 yeast
¼ cup lukewarm water
2 cups milk, scalded
¼ cup molasses
2 tablespoons sugar*

*¼ cup shortening
2 teaspoons salt
3 cups wheat flour
2 cups cornmeal
about 1 cup rye flour*

Mix the flours together. Follow the instructions for Recipe #1, but let rise only twice before kneading. Dust the kneading board with rye flour.

VARIATION: Add 1 cup chopped dates

RECIPE #3

RYE BREAD

*1 package (or cake)
  yeast*
¼ cup lukewarm water
2 cups milk, scalded
1 tablespoon sugar

*2 tablespoons
  shortening*
2 teaspoons salt
About 6 cups rye flour

Start the yeast, scald and cool the milk, mix in the
sugar, shortening and salt, add the yeast and stir
well, then add 2 cups flour and beat until smooth.
Cover and let rise for about an hour, until light
and bubbly. Add another 3 cups of flour and beat
well. Sprinkle a board with another cup of flour
and knead the dough well for 10 minutes, adding a
little more flour if needed. Divide into 2 parts,
shape into round loaves, place on a well-greased
baking sheet, cover, and let rise for about 2 hours,
until about double in bulk. Bake at 350° for about
an hour.

RECIPE #4

RUSSIAN-STYLE BLACK BREAD

2 packages (or cakes)
   yeast
½ cup lukewarm water
2 cups milk, scalded
2 tablespoons
   shortening
1 oz. (square)
   unsweetened baking
   chocolate

¼ cup molasses
1 tablespoon instant
   coffee
1 tablespoon salt
5 cups rye flour mixed
   with 1 cup cornmeal
1 tablespoon caraway
   seed

Start the yeast. Scald the milk and melt in it the shortening, chocolate, molasses and instant coffee. Cool and stir in the yeast and salt. Add about 2 cups of flour and the caraway seed, and beat until smooth. Add the rest of the flour. If the dough is still thin enough to beat with a spoon, add more flour to make it stiff and sticky. Cover with a clean cloth and let rise until double in bulk, about 2 hours. Punch down, turn dough out on a floured board, cover with cloth and let rest for 10 minutes. Knead for at least 10 minutes, dusting with rye flour, until dough becomes less sticky and rather elastic. Form into two round loaves, set on a well-greased baking sheet, cover, and let rise for about an hour. Bake for 15 minutes in a preheated 450° oven, then reduce the heat to 350° and bake until done, about 30 minutes more. To make the tops of the loaves shiny, brush with a little egg white beaten in a little water (do this just before baking, and again after about half an hour in the oven.

RECIPE #5

PUMPERNICKEL

2 packages (or cakes)
    yeast
1½ cups lukewarm
    water
1 cup molasses
2 tablespoons caraway
    seeds

1 tablespoon salt
2 cups rye flour mixed
    with 4 cups wheat
    flour
3 tablespoons
    shortening

Start the yeast in the 1½ cups of water. When softened and active, pour it into your mixing bowl and add the molasses, caraway seeds, and salt, and mix together. Add about half the flour and beat well. Beat in the shortening, which should be soft. Add the rest of the flour, turn out of the bowl, and knead for about 10 minutes, until smooth and elastic. Wash and butter the bowl, and put the dough in it. Cover and let the dough rise for about 2 hours, until double in bulk. Punch down, turn out onto a floured board, cover and let rest for 10 minutes. Shape into two loaves and put them in well-greased bread pans. Cover and let rise for about an hour. Bake in a preheated 450° oven for 15 minutes; then reduce heat to 350° and bake for about 30 minutes more.

RECIPE #6

OAT-RYE-WHEAT BREAD

1 package (or cake)
  yeast
½ cup lukewarm water
1 cup uncooked rolled
  oats
2 cups milk, scalded
¼ cup shortening

½ cup brown sugar
2 teaspoons salt
2 eggs, slightly beaten
1 cup wheat germ
2 cups rye flour
About 5 cups wheat
  flour

Start the yeast. Put the rolled oats in the mixing bowl and pour the scalded milk over them. Stir in the shortening, sugar and salt. When the mixture has cooled to lukewarm, stir in the yeast and the eggs. Add the wheat germ and rye flour and mix well. Then add enough wheat flour to make a workable dough. Turn out and knead for at least 5 minutes. Let rise. Shape into 2 loaves and place in well-greased bread pans. Let rise again and bake at 350° for about 45 minutes.

RECIPE #7

PORTUGUESE CORNBREAD

2 packages (or cakes)
  yeast
½ cup lukewarm water
3 cups cornmeal
2 cups boiling water

2 teaspoons salt
2 tablespoons olive oil
About 4 cups wheat
  flour

Start the yeast with a little sugar. Put 2 cups of the cornmeal and the salt in your mixing bowl and pour the boiling water over them, stirring constantly until smooth. Stir in the olive oil and let cool. When lukewarm, stir in the yeast, then mix in the cornmeal and as much wheat flour as you can work in with a spoon (about 3½ cups). Let rise until double in bulk, about an hour. Punch down, turn out, and knead for 5 minutes, working in a little more wheat flour as needed. Shape the dough into two flat round loaves and put them in well-greased 9″ pie pans. Let rise. Bake at 350° for about 40 minutes.

RECIPE #8

HOLIDAY WHEAT BREAD

*1 package (cake)
  yeast*
¼ cup lukewarm water
*1 cup scalded milk,
  cooled*
¾ cup butter
⅓ cup sugar
1 teaspoon salt

*1 teaspoon grated
  lemond rind*
pinch of cloves
*About 5 cups wheat
  flour*
1 cup chopped walnuts
1½ cups raisins

Start the yeast. Cream the butter and sugar, and beat in the eggs. Stir in the sugar, salt, lemon rind and cloves. Add the milk (cooled to lukewarm) and the yeast. Gradually beat in enough flour to make a workable dough. Work in the nuts and raisins. Turn out the dough and knead for at least 5 minutes, adding a little more flour as needed. Let rise until double in bulk, about an hour. Punch down, turn out onto a floured board, and let rest for 10 minutes. Shape in any way you wish—into buns, into small rings, or a large braided ring. Or try this:

Divide the dough into 13 pieces, one a little larger than the others. Form each piece into a long strand. Braid 5 strands together for the base, moistening the ends with egg white so they'll stick together. Then braid four strands and center on top of the first layer, then three more strands for the third layer. Stretch the last strand (the larger one) to twice the length of the others, double it over, and twist it for the top layer. Hold the loaf together with tooth picks. Let it rise for about an hour. Bake at 350° for about 40 minutes. Glaze or cover with powdered sugar. This is a very impressive braided loaf that dresses up any holiday table.

RECIPE #9

RAISED COFFEE CAKE

Plain wheat bread dough
Fruit or cheese topping

When you make wheat bread, you can bake one loaf of bread and use the remaining dough for coffee cake. Grease two 8″ round or square pans and press a thin layer of dough into the bottom of the pans. Prick the dough with a fork and let it rest for a few minutes. Then pinch up the edges to form a rim around the pan. Brush the surface with melted butter or a little egg white beaten with a little water. Cover the whole cake with a filling— cored, sliced apples; sliced fresh peaches; seeded cherries or plums; well-drained crushed pineapple; cheese filling. Top with sugar and cinnamon, or streusel.

Cheese filling. .
Put 1½ cups cottage cheese through the blender or ricer. Mix with ¼ cup sugar and a slightly beaten egg yolk. Beat an egg white until stiff and fold in.

Streusel
Rub together 2 tablespoons wheat flour, 2 tablespoons butter, 5 tablespoons sugar, until well mixed.

CHAPTER VI

QUICK BREADS, MUFFINS, BISCUITS

INTRODUCTION

Quick breads are so named because they rise with baking powder or soda as they bake, and so are much, much quicker to make than yeast breads.

The sweet quick breads and coffee cakes have been given a separate chapter as Breakfast Breads (Chapter II), because they're most popular for breakfast or as a mid-morning snack. The various breads in this chapter are good for breakfast too, of course, but are most commonly found as a side dish on the dinner table, or as part of a soup-and-salad lunch.

Because they're so quick and easy to prepare, these breads make an excellent stretcher for a meal when you suddenly have an unexpected person at the table ... and a hot, freshly baked bread makes any meal a little more festive.

COOKING AND SERVING: QUICK BREADS

Quick breads should be mixed lightly but thoroughly—too much mixing can make them heavy. They're best when served warm from the oven.

Time them so that breads baked in square or loaf pans will be done about 15 minutes before you want to serve them—they'll be much easier to cut and handle if they cool for a few minutes first.

Breads baked in flat pans should be cut into small squares and piled on a decorative plate to serve. Loaves can be served on a small cutting board with a knife alongside. At dinner, have butter on the table with hot breads. For a light lunch, you may also want to serve honey or colorful jelly.

RECIPES

RECIPE #1

PLAIN CORNBREAD

2 cups milk
1 cup cornmeal
2 tablespoons
  shortening

2 eggs
1 teaspoon salt
1 teaspoon baking
  powder

Mix the cornmeal with the milk in a saucepan, and bring just to the boiling point. Add the shortening and beat until smooth, then cool. Beat the eggs well, and add them and the baking powder and salt to the cooled cornmeal mixture. Bake in a greased 8″ square pan at 425° for 20 to 25 minutes.

RECIPE #2

SWEET CORNBREAD

1 cup cornmeal
1 cup wheat flour
½ cup sugar
4 teaspoons baking
  powder

½ teaspoon salt
1 egg
1 cup milk
¼ cup melted
  shortening

Mix together the cornmeal, flour, sugar, baking powder, and salt. Beat the egg into the milk, add the shortening, and mix the liquid into the dry ingredients lightly but thoroughly. Bake in a greased 8″ or 9″ square pan at 425° for 20 to 25 minutes.

RECIPE #3

WHEAT GERM CORNBREAD

This is a delicious, very nutritious variation of Sweet Cornbread, RECIPE #2.

Add 1 cup wheat germ to the dry ingredients; substitute ½ cup honey for the sugar; use 1½ cups milk instead of 1 cup. Bake in a greased 9″ x 13″ pan at 425° for 20 to 25 minutes.

RECIPE #4

BUTTERMILK CORNBREAD

1 cup cornmeal
1 cup wheat flour
1 teaspoon baking
  powder
½ teaspoon soda
2 tablespoons brown
  sugar

½ teaspoon salt
2 eggs
1 cup buttermilk
4 tablespoons melted
  shortening

Mix together the cornmeal, flour, baking powder, soda, sugar and salt. Beat the eggs well, mix into the buttermilk and melted shortening. Stir the liquid into the dry ingredients lightly but thoroughly. Bake in a greased 8″ square pan at 425° for about 20 minutes.

RECIPE #5

PARAGUAYAN CORNBREAD

1½ cups cornmeal	1½ cups corn (fresh or
1½ cups grated	canned) kernels
Muenster cheese	3 eggs
1 teaspoon salt	⅔ cup milk
½ cup coarsely chopped	¼ cup olive oil (or
onions	melted shortening)

Mix together the cornmeal, grated cheese and salt. Saute the onions until they are translucent and soft, and add them to the cornmeal mixture. Puree the corn in a blender, and add to the cornmeal mixture. Separate the eggs. Beat the yolks, mix them with the milk and shortening, and mix into the dry ingredients lightly but thoroughly. Beat the egg whites until stiff, and fold them into the rest of the batter. Pour the batter into a well-greased 9″ square pan, dusted with Parmesan cheese or cornmeal. Dot the top with butter, and bake at 325° for about 45 minutes.

RECIPE #6

CORN PONE

2 cups cornmeal	1 teaspoon soda
1 teaspoon salt	1½ cups buttermilk
1 teaspoon sugar	

Mix together the cornmeal, salt, sugar, and soda. Stir in the buttermilk until well mixed. Drop by spoonfuls into a little melted shortening in a skillet, and fry covered over low heat until brown on both sides, 20 to 25 minutes.

RECIPE #7

HOE CAKE

2 cups cornmeal   hot water
½ teaspoon salt   cold water

Put the cornmeal and salt into a mixing bowl and add enough hot water to make a stiff batter (about a cup). Moisten your hands with cold water, form a tablespoon of batter into a cake, and bake like a griddle cake on a hot griddle or skillet (use a little grease if necessary) until brown on both sides.

RECIPE #8

CORN ZEPHYRS

1 cup cornmeal   4 cups boiling water
1 teaspoon salt   4 egg whites
1 tablespoon
   shortening

Put the cornmeal, salt, shortening in a saucepan. Pour the boiling water over them and cook in a double boiler for 30 minutes, stirring frequently. Cool. Beat the egg whites until stiff. Fold into the cornmeal mixture and drop from a spoon onto a greased baking sheet. Bake at 350° for about 30 minutes.

About 20 puffs

RECIPE #9

CORN PUFFS

1 cup cornmeal	2 tablespoons
1 tablespoon sugar	shortening
1 teaspoon salt	2 cups boiling water
	2 eggs

Put the cornmeal, sugar, salt and shortening in a saucepan and pour the boiling water over them. Cook, stirring frequently, until the mixture thickens into a thick mush. Separate the egg whites until stiff, and fold into the batter. Drop from a spoon onto a greased baking sheet. Bake at 425° for about 20 minutes.

About 20 puffs

RECIPE #10

CORN DODGERS

1 cup cornmeal	1 tablespoon
1 teaspoon salt	shortening
1 tablespoon sugar	1 cup boiling water
	1 egg

Put the cornmeal, salt, sugar and shortening into a mixing bowl, pour the boiling water over them and mix well. Cool. Beat the egg and beat into the cooled batter. Drop from a spoon onto a greased baking sheet. Bake at 400° for about 20 minutes.

About 25 cakes

RECIPE #11

CORN AND GRAHAM JOHNNYCAKE

2 cups cornmeal
2 cups graham flour
2 teaspoons soda
1 teaspoon salt
2 eggs

⅓ cup molasses
2 tablespoons melted
  shortening
3 cups buttermilk

Mix together the cornmeal, flour, soda and salt. Beat the eggs, and mix in the molasses, shortening and buttermilk. Stir the liquid into the dry ingredients and beat well. Bake in a greased 9" x 13" pan at 400° for 20 to 25 minutes.

RECIPE #12

HONEY JOHNNYCAKE

2 cups cornmeal
½ cup wheat flour
1 teaspoon soda
2 eggs

2 tablespoons melted
  butter
¼ cup honey
2 cups buttermilk

Mix the cornmeal, flour, and soda together. Beat the eggs, then beat in the shortening, honey and buttermilk. Beat the dry ingredients into the liquid, a little at a time. Pour the batter into a greased 9" square pan and bake at 425° for about 20 minutes.

RECIPE #13

PLAIN WHEAT BUNS

½ cup sugar
½ cup butter
3 cups wheat flour
½ cup milk
1 egg yolk

2 teaspoons baking
  powder
¼ teaspoon lemon
  extract

Cream the butter and sugar and mix in the flour and baking powder. Warm the milk to lukewarm, mix in the egg yolk and lemon extract, and stir the liquid into the flour mixture. Beat well, until smooth. Put small pieces of the dough into greased muffin tins and bake at 425° for about 25 minutes.

Variation: Put tiny balls of dough into each muffin cup for a cloverleaf roll.

About 12 buns

RECIPE #14

CURRANT BREAD

3 cups flour
½ teaspoon baking
  powder
½ teaspoon soda

4 tablespoons
  shortening
4 tablespoons sugar
1 cup currants or raisins
1 egg
1 cup milk

Mix together the flour, baking powder, soda and sugar. Rub in the shortening, and stir in the currants. Beat the egg well into the milk, then mix the liquid into the dry ingredients lightly but thoroughly. Pour into a greased 9″ square pan and bake at 350° for about 30 minutes.

RECIPE #15

FLAT ONION BREAD

6 tablespoons melted
 shortening
1½ cups finely chopped
 onions

¾ cup lukewarm water
1 teaspoon salt
2½ to 3 cups wheat or
 rye flour

Saute the onions in a little of the melted shortening until they are translucent and tender. Stir in the water and salt and 2½ cups of flour, beat well. Add enough more flour to make a dough that doesn't stick to your fingers. With your hands, shape the dough into 2-inch balls and roll out with a lightly floured rolling pin into flat circles. Fry each circle like a griddle cake on an ungreased griddle or skillet until brown on both sides.

About 16 8" breads

RECIPE #16

BUCKWHEAT HOT BREAD

1 cup buckwheat
 flour
½ cup wheat flour
1 teaspoon baking
 powder
½ teaspoon soda

½ teaspoon salt
½ cup brown sugar
¾ cup buttermilk
¼ cup sour cream
1 egg

Mix together the flours, baking powder, soda, salt, and sugar. Beat the egg and mix in the buttermilk and sour cream. Stir the liquids into the dry ingredients lightly but thoroughly. Bake in a greased 8" or 9" square pan at 350° for about 20 minutes.

RECIPE #17

OATMEAL CAKES

2 cups rolled oats   2 tablespoons
1 teaspoon salt   shortening
                            about ¾ cup water

Rub the shortening into the oatmeal and salt. Add
enough cold water to make a thick dough. Mix
until smooth. Roll out thin and cut into rounds or
squares. Bake on an ungréased baking sheet at
425° for 8 to 10 minutes.

RECIPE #18

CORNMEAL SCONES

You need muffin rings to make these authentic.

2 cups cornmeal   1 tablespoon sugar
2 teaspoons baking   1 tablespoon shortening
   powder   about 1 cup milk
1 teaspoon salt

Mix together the cornmeal, baking powder, salt
and sugar. Rub in the shortening. Mix in enough
milk to make a fairly stiff batter. Drop into muffin
rings on a fairly hot griddle and bake until
browned on both sides.

COOKING AND SERVING: MUFFINS

The perfect muffin is light and moist, slightly rounded on top, with a rather coarse but even texture. The secret of making perfect muffins is not to beat the batter. Muffin batter is mixed very lightly, for a few seconds only—just enough to moisten the dry ingredients, without making any attempt to get rid of all of the lumps. Once mixed, the batter should be transferred to greased muffin tins—filling each cup about ⅔ full—and baked at once.

Serve muffins hot out of the oven, wrapped in a napkin in a breadbasket. (They can be warmed over, if necessary—wrap them in foil, or in a lightly moistened brown paper bag, and warm them for a few minutes in a hot oven.)

Muffins are perfect for dinner with only a little butter, and equally appropriate for breakfast and lunch with honey, jam, etc. as well.

RECIPE #19

CORNMEAL RICE BREAD

This should bake in a hot greased skillet, but a hot greased square baking pan will do.

1 cup cornmeal
1 tablespoon sugar
1 tablespoon baking
  powder
1 teaspoon salt

4 tablespoons wheat
  flour
1 cup boiled rice
2 cups milk

Mix everything together thoroughly. The batter should be fairly runny. Pour into a hot greased skillet or baking pan, and bake at 400° for about 45 minutes.

RECIPE #20

WHEAT MUFFINS

1½ cups wheat flour
1 teaspoon salt
2 teaspoons baking
  powder
1 egg

1 cup milk
1 tablespoon melted
  shortening
2 tablespoons molasses

Mix together the flour, salt and baking powder. Beat the egg well, mix with the milk, melted shortening and molasses. Stir the liquid into the dry ingredients very lightly. Bake at 400° for about 20 minutes.

About 20 muffins

RECIPE #21

EGGLESS BUTTERMILK MUFFINS

2 cups wheat flour
¼ cup brown sugar
1 teaspoon salt
1 teaspoon soda

¾ teaspoon baking
  powder
4 tablespoons melted
  shortening
1½ cups buttermilk

Mix together the flour, sugar, salt, soda and baking powder. Mix the shortening with the buttermilk, and stir the liquid into the dry ingredients very lightly. Bake at 400° for about 20 minutes.

About 25 muffins

RECIPE #22

WHEAT RICE MUFFINS

1 cup flour
1 tablespoon sugar
1 teaspoon salt
1 teaspoon baking
  powder

¾ cup boiled rice
1 egg
2 tablespoons melted
  shortening
1½ cups milk

Mix together the flour, salt, sugar and baking powder. Add the rice. Beat the egg and mix it with the shortening and milk. Stir the liquid into the dry ingredients very lightly. Bake at 400° for 15 or 20 minutes.

18 to 20 muffins

RECIPE #23

HONEY CURRANT MUFFINS

4 tablespoons shortening	1 cup wheat flour
6 tablespoons honey	4 teaspoons baking powder
2 eggs	1 teaspoon salt
½ cup currants	1½ cups milk

Cream the butter and honey. Beat the egg and add gradually to the butter mixture, beating it well. Stir in the currants, then add the flour, baking powder and salt alternately with the milk, mixing lightly. Bake at 375° for 15 to 20 minutes.

RECIPE #24

BRAN MUFFINS

2 cups wheat flour	1 egg
1½ cups bran	2 cups buttermilk
2 tablespoons brown sugar	½ cup molasses
¼ teaspoon soda	4 tablespoons melted shortening
½ teaspoon salt	

Mix together the flour, bran, brown sugar, soda and salt. Beat the egg, and mix it with the buttermilk, molasses and shortening. Stir the liquid into the dry ingredients very lightly. Bake at 350° for about 25 minutes.

VARIATION: Fold in 1 cup raisins and/or nuts with the last mixing.

About 24 muffins

RECIPE #25

HONEY BRAN MUFFINS

2 cups wheat flour
2 cups bran
4 teaspoons baking
   powder
1 teaspoon salt
1 cup chopped nuts

1 egg
¾ cup honey
2 tablespoons melted
   shortening
2 cups milk

Mix together the flour, bran, baking powder, salt and nuts. Beat an egg and mix it with the honey, shortening and milk. Stir the liquid into the dry ingredients very lightly. Bake at 400° for about 30 minutes.

About 24 muffins

RECIPE #26

CORN MUFFINS

2 cups cornmeal
1 cup wheat flour
1 teaspoon salt
1 tablespoon sugar
2 teaspoons baking
   powder

1 egg
1 cup milk
2 tablespoons melted
   shortening

Mix together the cornmeal, flour, salt, sugar and baking powder. Beat the egg and mix it with the milk and melted shortening. Stir the liquid into the dry ingredients very lightly. Bake at 400° for 20 to 25 minutes.

About 20 muffins

RECIPE #27

OATMEAL MUFFINS

1 cup buttermilk
1 cup rolled oats
1 cup wheat flour
½ teaspoon soda
1 teaspoon baking
  powder

2 tablespoons sugar
1 teaspoon salt
1 egg
¼ cup melted
  shortening

Heat the buttermilk to scalding and pour it on the rolled oats and let stand for 10 minutes. Mix together the flour, soda, baking powder, sugar and salt. Beat the egg, add the shortening, and mix into the oatmeal mixture. Add the oatmeal mixture to the dry ingredients and stir very lightly. Bake at 425° for about 20 minutes.

About 15 muffins

RECIPE #28

BUCKWHEAT MUFFINS

2 cups buckwheat flour
1 teaspoon salt
1 teaspoon soda
1 tablespoon sugar

1 egg
2 cups buttermilk
2 tablespoons melted
  shortening

Mix together the flour, salt, soda and sugar. Beat the egg and add it to the buttermilk and melted shortening. Mix the liquid into the dry ingredients very lightly. Bake at 400° for about 20 minutes.

About 15 muffins

RECIPE #29

RYE MUFFINS

1 cup rye flour	1 egg
1/4 cup wheat flour	1 cup milk
1 teaspoon salt	4 tablespoons melted
1 teaspoon baking	shortening
powder	2 tablespoons molasses
1/2 teaspoon soda	

Mix together the flours, salt, baking powder and soda. Beat the egg and mix it with the milk, shortening and molasses. Stir the liquid into the dry ingredients very lightly. Bake at 425° for about 20 minutes.

About 12 to 15 muffins

RECIPE #30

RYE AND WHEAT MUFFINS

1 cup rye flour	1/2 teaspoon salt
1 cup wheat flour	2 eggs
1/4 cup sugar	1 cup milk
1 teaspoon baking	1/4 cup melted
powder	shortening
1/2 teaspoon soda	

Mix together the flours, sugar, baking powder, soda and salt. Beat the eggs, mix with the milk and shortening and stir the liquid into the dry ingredients very lightly. Bake at 425° for about 20 minutes.

About 15 muffins

RECIPE #31

PORRIDGE MUFFINS

1½ cups wheat flour
1 tablespoon sugar
½ teaspoon salt
2 teaspoons baking
  powder
2 eggs

1¼ cups milk
2 tablespoons melted
  shortening
1 cup leftover breakfast
  porridge (any kind)

Mix together the flour, sugar, salt and baking powder. Separate the eggs. Beat the yolks and mix them with the milk, shortening, and porridge. Stir the porridge mixture into the dry ingredients very lightly. Beat the egg whites until stiff and fold them into the rest of the batter. Bake at 400° for about 25 minutes.

About 30 muffins

RECIPE #32

MIXED GRAIN MUFFINS

½ cup wheat flour
½ cup rye flour
½ cup cornmeal
2 tablespoons sugar
2 teaspoons baking
  powder

½ teaspoon salt
1 cup milk
2 eggs
4 tablespoons melted
  shortening

Mix together the flours, cornmeal, sugar, baking powder, and salt. Beat the eggs, mix into the milk and shortening, and mix the liquid into the dry ingredients very lightly.

About 20 muffins

RECIPE #33

BLUEBERRY MUFFINS

1 cup cornmeal	1 egg
½ cup wheat flour	1 cup milk
2 teaspoons baking powder	4 tablespoons melted shortening
½ teaspoon salt	4 tablespoons honey
1 cup fresh blueberries or well-drained canned blueberries	

Mix together the cornmeal, flour, baking powder and salt. Fold in the blueberries. Beat the egg well, add to the milk, shortening and honey and mix well. Stir the liquid into the dry ingredients very lightly. Bake at 425° for about 20 minutes.

About 24 muffins

RECIPE #34

NUT MUFFINS

1 cup cornmeal	2 eggs
1 cup rye flour	1 cup milk
2 teaspoons baking powder	4 tablespoons melted shortening
½ teaspoon salt	4 tablespoons molasses
1 cup chopped nuts	

Mix together the cornmeal, flour, baking powder and salt. Stir in the nuts. Beat the eggs, mix in the milk, shortening and molasses thoroughly, and stir the liquid into the dry ingredients very lightly. Bake at 425° for about 20 minutes.

VARIATIONS: Substitute 1 cup of raisins for the nuts, or use ½ cup each raisins and nuts.

About 24 muffins

COOKING AND SERVING: BISCUITS

Biscuits come in many shapes and flavors, but all are light and flaky—a delicious accompaniment to stews, fried chicken or any hearty meal that includes a meat gravy.

Rolled biscuits begin with flour and solid shortening. The shortening is rubbed with the fingers, or cut with a pastry blender, into the flour until the mixture is about the texture of coarse cornmeal. Then the other ingredients are added, and enough liquid to make a fairly firm dough that can be rolled out with a rolling pin or patted out with your hands. Biscuits are usually cut with a 2-inch round cookie cutter, or shaped with your hands into 2-inch round cakes. The dough should be handled as little as possible to keep it light. Rolled biscuits are baked on an ungreased baking sheet.

Drop biscuits usually have more liquid and less shortening than rolled biscuits, and are made from a stiff, sticky batter that can be dropped from a spoon. They are usually crisper, but less rich and flaky than rolled biscuits.

Biscuits are traditionally served with butter and honey for lunch or dinner, and are delightful for breakfast too with marmalade or any sweet spread.

RECIPE #35

AUNT ANNE'S BAKING POWDER BISCUITS

This is a very simple recipe, which can be used with any kind of whole-grain flour.

For each cup of flour, use:

2 tablespoons shortening

2 teaspoons baking powder

about ½ teaspoon salt

about ⅓ cup milk

Rub or cut the shortening into the flour. Mix in the baking powder and salt. (NOTE: If you are using more than 2 cups of flour, don't increase the salt in proportion—add about ¼ teaspoon per cup, and taste the dough and adjust as necessary.) Mix in enough milk to make a fairly firm dough, turn out on a floured board and knead just enough so the dough doesn't stick. Roll or pat out about ¼" thick and cut with a cookie cutter or shape with your hands into 2-inch biscuits. Bake on an ungreased baking sheet at 450° for 12 to 15 minutes.

2 cups of flour makes about 12 wheat biscuits or 8 to 10 rye biscuits.

RECIPE #36

SOUR CREAM BISCUITS

2 cups wheat or
   buckwheat flour
1 teaspoon soda

1 teaspoon salt
¼ cup sour cream
about ¼ cup milk

Mix together the flour, soda and salt. Stir in the sour cream and enough milk to make a fairly firm dough. Turn out on floured board and knead just enough so the dough doesn't stick. Roll or pat out about ¼″ thick and cut with a cookie cutter or shape with your hands into 2-inch biscuits. Bake on an ungreased baking sheet at 450° for 12 to 15 minutes.

About 12 biscuits

RECIPE #37

BUTTERMILK BISCUITS

2 cups wheat,
   buckwheat or rye
   flour
1 teaspoon soda

½ teaspoon salt
2 tablespoons
   shortening
about ⅔ cup buttermilk

Rub or cut the shortening into the flour, mix in the soda and salt, and stir in enough buttermilk to make a fairly firm dough.

Proceed as in Recipe #35.

About 12 biscuits

RECIPE #38

RICH BUTTERMILK BISCUITS

2 cups wheat, buckwheat or rye flour	2 teaspoons baking powder
¼ cup shortening	½ teaspoon soda
1 teaspoon salt	2 teaspoons honey
	about ⅔ cup buttermilk

Rub or cut the shortening into the flour. Mix in the salt, baking powder and soda. Mix the honey with the buttermilk, and add enough liquid to the dry ingredients to make a fairly firm, light dough. Proceed as in Recipe #35.

About 18 biscuits

RECIPE #39

DROP BISCUITS

2 cups wheat flour	1 tablespoon baking powder
1 tablespoon sugar	¾ to 1 cup milk
½ teaspoon salt	

Mix together the flour, sugar, salt, and baking powder. Stir in ¾ cup milk, then enough to make a fairly stiff batter that will drop from a spoon. Drop biscuits about 2 inches apart on a greased baking sheet, and bake at 450° for 10 to 12 minutes.

15 to 18 biscuits

RECIPE #40

MOLASSES WHEAT BISCUITS

2 *cups wheat flour*
4 *tablespoons*
   shortening
1 *teaspoon soda*
3 *teaspoons baking*
   powder

1 *teaspoon salt*
2 *tablespoons*
   molasses
about ⅔ cup milk

Rub or cut the shortening into the flour, and mix in the soda, baking powder and salt. Stir the molasses into the milk, and add enough liquid to make a fairly firm dough. Proceed as in Recipe #35.

About 12 biscuits

RECIPE #41

RICH SHORTCAKE BISCUITS

2 *cups wheat flour*
¼ *cup shortening*
2½ *teaspoons baking*
   powder

1¼ *teaspoons salt*
2 *tablespoons sugar*
about ⅔ cup cream

Rub or cut the shortening into the flour. Mix in the baking powder, salt, and sugar. Stir in enough cream to make a fairly firm dough, and proceed as in Recipe #35.

About 15 biscuits, or 8 to 10 large shortcakes

CHAPTER VII

SIDE DISHES

INTRODUCTION

Every country, every culture, has its favorite "filler"—the common starchy food served with almost every meal. In America, in spite of the variety of cultures that have introduced their favorite foods into our way of life, we seem to have settled on the potato as our starch.

Here are some ways to add variety to your meals with whole-grain "fillers"—lots of ways to use rice, of course; some novel uses for cornmeal; and an assortment of other hearty, tasty dishes representing several nations.

And unless you normally eat your potatoes in their jackets, these good whole-grain recipes add nutrition to your meals, as well as some very appealing flavors.

RECIPE #1

HUSH PUPPIES

Deep-fried onion-flavored cornbread puffs, traditionally served with fried fish.

2 cups cornmeal
3 teaspoons baking
   powder
½ teaspoon salt

2 eggs
About ¾ cup buttermilk
1 medium onion,
   minced

Mix together the cornmeal, baking powder and salt. Beat the eggs well, and beat into the dry ingredients. Beat in enough buttermilk to make a light dough that keeps its shape in a spoon. Stir in the onion. Drop by spoonfuls (push off one spoon with a second spoon) into hot fat, and deep-fry for about 3 minutes, until golden brown. Serve hot, with butter.

About 24 puppies

RECIPE #2

POLENTA

An Italian cornmeal mush that can be served either in its porridge form, or chilled, sliced, and fried.

3 cups water
1 teaspoon salt
1 cup cornmeal

¾ cup grated sharp
    cheese (optional)

Boil the water and salt, and pour in the cornmeal slowly, stirring constantly, making sure the boiling never stops until the cornmeal is all in the water, and the mixture is smooth. Simmer, stirring frequently, for 20 to 30 minutes, until the consistency of thick porridge. Then stir in the cheese and serve at once. *Or* spread thin in a baking dish and chill until firm, then cut into squares, fry until warm through and serve hot, with the sauce from your meal.

Serves 4 to 6

RECIPE #3

PLAIN SPOON BREAD

2 cups milk	6 tablespoons
1 cup cornmeal	shortening
1 teaspoon salt	6 eggs

Heat the milk in a 2-quart saucepan until scalding, but not quite boiling. Pour in the cornmeal slowly, stirring constantly, and cook without boiling until thick and smooth. Add the salt and the shortening, broken into small bits, and stir until the shortening is melted and mixed in thoroughly. Separate the eggs, beating the yolks into the cornmeal mixture one at a time. Beat the egg whites until stiff. Stir about a third of the egg white into the batter, then fold in the rest gently but thoroughly. Pour the batter into a well-greased 1-quart baking dish and bake it at 375° for about 40 minutes, or until a knife stuck into the center comes out clean. Serve at once, directly from its dish.

6 generous servings

RECIPE #4

SPICY SPOON BREAD WITH FRESH CORN

3 or 4 ears of fresh
  corn
3 cups milk
2 teaspoons salt
1 cup cornmeal
½ cup shortening

3 eggs
1 tablespoon sugar
¼ teaspoon ground
  nutmeg
¼ teaspoon cayenne
  pepper

Grate the corn on the large holes of a hand grater.
Mix the grated corn and its liquid with 2 cups of
the milk and the salt, and bring to a boil. Pour in
the cornmeal slowly, stirring constantly, until it's
all mixed in and the mixture is smooth. Simmer,
stirring frequently, until quite thick. Remove from
the heat and add the shortening, a little at a time,
until it's all melted and mixed in. Beat in the rest of
the milk and mix thoroughly. Separate the eggs,
and beat the yolks into the batter one at a time.
Beat in the sugar, nutmeg and pepper. Beat the egg
whites until stiff, then fold into the batter. Spread
in a greased 2-quart baking dish and bake at 350°
for about 40 minutes, until the center barely
moves when the dish is moved gently. Serve at
once, directly from the baking dish.

6 or 8 servings

RECIPE #5

PERFECT BOILED RICE

This one has never failed, and makes us wonder why so many cooks consider rice a mystery.

2 cups water
½ teaspoon salt

1½ teaspoons
shortening
1 cup rice

Put the water, salt and shortening into a saucepan and bring to a boil. Pour in the rice, stirring until it's all mixed in to prevent lumps. Bring to a boil again and stir well once more. Cover, reduce the heat to simmer, and leave it alone for 20 minutes. Lift the lid and it should be perfect—if it's still a little watery, simmer for 3 to 5 minutes more.

VARIATIONS: 1. Use stock instead of water. 2. Add 1 tablespoon dried soup vegetables. 3. Add ½ teaspoon of any herb you like.

Serves 4 to 6

RECIPE #6

SWEET BUTTERED RICE

Delicious with curries, or any spicy dish—good as breakfast cereal, too.

½ cup rice
1½ cups milk
4 tablespoons butter

about 4 tablespoons
* sugar*
½ teaspoon nutmeg or
1½ teaspoons cinnamon

Put the rice and milk in a saucepan and simmer, stirring occasionally, until the rice is tender (about 45 minutes). Pour off any excess milk and save it. Return the rice to the heat, and stir in the butter, sugar, and spice (use more or less sugar to suit your taste). Serve hot. If you have some left over, refrigerate it overnight, and in the morning, reheat the leftover milk, pour it on the rice, and serve as hot cereal.

4 or 5 servings

RECIPE #7

RICE MOLD

This makes a rice ring that you can fill with any colorful creamed or mixed main dish or vegetable, for a beautiful display. And it's very easy!

2 cups water	1 cup rice
½ teaspoon salt	½ teaspoon grated
1½ teaspoons	nutmeg
shortening	¼ cup melted butter

Boil the rice, following directions for Recipe #5. Stir in the nutmeg. Press the rice into a well-greased 7-inch ring mold. Pour the melted butter over it, set it in a pan of hot water, and bake at 350° for about 20 minutes. Loosen the edges and turn out onto a platter. Fill the center with any colorful or creamed dish.

VARIATIONS: Use broth instead of water (if it's salty, don't add the salt called for), and use an herb—thyme, sage, etc.—instead of the nutmeg. Before pressing the rice into the mold, you can add bits of pimento, and/or about ½ cup frozen green peas, slightly cooked.

Serves 6

RECIPE #8

PLAIN RICE PILAF

½ cup chopped onion
¼ cup shortening
2 cups chicken, beef or
  other broth

1 cup vegetable bits or
  chopped meat
  (optional)

In a 10″ or 12″ skillet, saute the onion in the shortening until translucent and tender. Stir in the rice until it's all coated with oil. Add the broth, stirring so the rice won't stick. Bring to a boil and stir again. Add the vegetables or meat, if you like (this is a good way to use up leftover bits). Cover, reduce heat, and simmer for 20 minutes, or until all the liquid is absorbed. Serve hot.

Serves 4 to 6

RECIPE #9

HONEY-FRUIT PILAF

Excellent with spicy curries.

2 tablespoons currants
4 prunes
¼ cup dried apricots
4 tablespoons
  shortening

¼ cup finely chopped
  blanched almonds
2 tablespoons honey
1 cup rice
2 cups water

Slice the prunes and apricots into narrow strips. Soak the prunes and currants until they begin to soften (about 15 minutes). In a 10″ or 12″ skillet, melt the shortening. Add the apricots, currants, prunes and almonds, and cook over low heat, uncovered, for about 5 minutes. Stir in the honey and rice, add 2 cups of water, and stir well so the rice doesn't stick. Bring to a boil, stir once again, cover, reduce heat and simmer for about 20 minutes, or until the water is absorbed. Serve hot.

Serves 4 to 6

RECIPE #10

CHINESE-STYLE FRIED RICE

This is a good lunch dish, or perfect for dinner with any Oriental or Polynesian style entree.

Perfect Boiled Rice (Recipe #5)
¼ cup shortening
2 tablespoons minced scallions
½ teaspoon salt

½ cup meat (thin-sliced pork, diced shrimp, thin-sliced beef, etc.)
2 eggs
about 2 tablespoons soy sauce

Saute the rice in the shortening until it starts to turn golden brown. Stir in the scallions, salt and meat. When well mixed, scrape everything to the sides of the skillet so there's a bare spot in the center. Break in the eggs, scramble them until they just start to harden, then stir them into the rice. Add a tablespoon of soy sauce, stir in well, and taste—then add more soy sauce to taste. Serve hot.

4 generous servings

RECIPE #11

RICE AND BEANS

1 cup dried black beans
about 10 cups water
4 tablespoons
 shortening
¼ cup diced salt pork
2 cloves garlic, minced
½ cup onions, finely
 chopped

¼ cup green pepper,
 finely chopped
1½ cups rice
1½ teaspoons salt
Fresh ground black
 pepper

Wash the beans, and put them in a 3 or 4 quart saucepan with 7 cups of water. Bring to a boil, reduce heat, and simmer, covered, for 2½ to 3 hours. Stir occasionally, and add more water if necessary. The beans are ready when they're tender but still intact. Drain the beans, and mash 2 tablespoons of them into a smooth paste. Set aside. In a heavy 10″ or 12″ skillet, fry the salt pork in the shortening until the pork bits are crisp and brown. Skim out the bits and drain them; add the garlic, onions and pepper to the shortening and cook until the onions are transparent, about 5 minutes. Stir in the bean paste, then add the beans and pork bits. Reduce heat and simmer, uncovered, for 10 minutes. Add the rice, salt, and 2 cups of water and stir well. Bring to a boil and stir again. Cover, reduce heat, and simmer for about 20 minutes, until all the water is absorbed. Season to taste with salt and pepper, and serve hot.

8 to 10 servings

RECIPE #12

RICE CROQUETTES

1 cup rice	*flavoring*
3 cups milk	*1 egg, well beaten*
¾ cup powdered sugar	*dried bread crumbs*

Put the rice, milk and sugar in a saucepan and simmer gently until all the milk is absorbed, about 45 minutes. Stir in ¼ teaspoon vanilla, lemon extract, almond extract, or any other flavoring you like. Cool the rice, then form it into small round balls. Dip each ball into the beaten egg, cover with bread crumbs, and deep-fry for about 10 minutes, until golden brown.

8 or 10 croquettes

RECIPE #13

KASHA

1 cup kasha	*1 tablespoon*
(buckwheat groats)	*shortening*
1 egg	*1 teaspoon salt*
2 to 3 cups water	

Toast the dry kasha in a deep skillet, stirring constantly. Break in the egg and stir in well, until all the glisten is gone. Add 2 cups of water and the salt and shortening. Bring to a boil, stir and cover. Reduce heat and simmer for 20 minutes, and taste. If the kasha is dry, add another cup of water and simmer for 10 minutes more, until the kasha is tender and the water is absorbed. Serve hot.

4 or 5 servings

RECIPE #14

KASHA WITH MUSHROOMS

1 cup kasha
1 egg
2 to 3 cups water
1 tablespoon shortening
1 teaspoon salt
2 cups finely chopped
   onions

½ pound fresh
   mushrooms, finely
   chopped
4 tablespoons
   shortening

With the first five ingredients, follow instructions for Recipe #13. Melt half the remaining shortening in a skillet. Add the onions and simmer until translucent, about 5 minutes. Stir the onions into the kasha. Melt the remaining shortening, add the mushrooms, and cook for 2 to 3 minutes over medium heat, stirring frequently. Then turn up the heat to high and cook the mushrooms, uncovered, until all the liquid in the pan has evaporated. Toss the mushrooms into the kasha, season to taste with salt and pepper, and serve at once.

6 to 8 servings

RECIPE #15

SAVORY BARLEY

2 quarts water
1½ tablespoons salt
1 cup barley
4 tablespoons
  shortening

1 large onion, diced
4 stalks celery, diced
  (use the leaves, too)
½ tablespoon poultry
  seasoning

Bring the water to a boil in a large kettle. Add the salt, then stir in the barley. Reduce heat and simmer until the barley is tender, about 40 minutes. Drain the barley and set it aside. In a skillet, melt the shortening, and stir in the onions, celery and poultry seasoning. Cook, stirring occasionally, until the onions are translucent, about 5 minutes. Mix into the barley thoroughly, and serve hot.

6 to 8 servings

RECIPE #16

LIGHT WHEAT DUMPLINGS

These are great for lunch with soup, or for dinner, on the day you're baking bread.

*Plain Wheat Bread
  Dough (Page 64) or
  any other bread
  dough you like*

Boiling water

At the point when you're shaping the bread dough into loaves, set aside some for dumplings. Cover it and let it rise a little (about 15 minutes), then gently shape it into balls about the size of a golf ball. Drop them into the boiling water, and boil them for 20 minutes. They must be eaten immediately, or they fall. Serve with any meat sauce, or with butter.

CHAPTER VIII

COOKIES

INTRODUCTION

Cookies are fun—fun to make and fun to eat. They come in all shapes, all sizes, all flavors. There are big cookies for the children's lunchbox or the cookie jar—tiny cookies for tea—fancy cookies for holidays or gifts.

Cookies and children seem to go together. Many an infant cuts his teeth on a hard sweet biscuit, almost every toddler loves to chew on a cookie as he explores his new world, the cookie jar often is the first stop when the school child comes home, and the youngest cook in the kitchen almost invariably wants to start his career by baking cookies. So it's natural that concerned mothers are looking for ways to make this universal favorite as nutritious as possible.

This chapter presents many old favorites invigorated with the addition of good whole-grain flours and natural honey ... recipes every bit as tasty as—and a good deal more nourishing than almost anything on the market today. You can make any of these recipes still more nutritious by adding ¼ to ½ cup soy flour, non-fat dry milk solids and/or wheat germ. If this makes the dough a little dry, simply add another tablespoon of shortening or liquid.

ABOUT COOKIES

The common kinds of cookies are drop, rolled, molded, refrigerator and bar.

Drop cookies are made from a dough thin enough to drop from a spoon onto a cookie sheet; *rolled cookies* are made from a stiff dough that's rolled out thin with a rolling pin and cut into shapes with a cookie cutter; *molded cookies* are made from a rather stiff dough that's shaped with the hands; *refrigerator cookies* are usually quite rich and are chilled overnight in long rolls, then sliced with a sharp knife before baking; *bar cookies* are baked like a quick bread in a flat pan, then sliced into squares or bars before they cool.

Cookies (except bar cookies) usually bake quite quickly in a moderately hot oven. Unless your oven keeps perfectly even temperature (most don't), you should turn the cookie sheets and change them from top to the bottom shelf, and vice versa if you're using two—about halfway through the cooking period. This takes a little extra attention, but it will prevent part of the cookies starting to burn before the others are quite done.

Except for bar cookies, all cookies bake best on a flat cookie sheet without sides, which permits the heat to reach all parts of the cookies freely—and also makes it much easier to remove them from the pan.

When cookies come out of the oven, set the sheets on a cooking rack and let them begin to cook before you try to handle them. Otherwise, they're apt to break and crumble. When they're cool enough to handle, lift them with a spatula and set them on a cooling rack in a single layer. Let them cool thoroughly before storing them.

RECIPES

RECIPE #1

AUSTRALIAN NUGGETS

6 tablespoons sweet
  butter
3 tablespoons honey

¼ teaspoon salt
½ teaspoon vanilla
1 cup wheat flour

Melt the butter and honey, and stir in the salt and vanilla. Beat in the flour until well mixed. Flour your hands and shape the dough into 1-inch balls. Place them on a greased baking sheet, press the center of each ball with your thumb and bake at 350° for about 15 minutes.

About 24 nuggets

RECIPE #2

BRAN CAKES

2 cups wheat flour	2 eggs
1 teaspoon baking powder	¾ teaspoon soda
	1 teaspoon vanilla
1 teaspoon cinnamon	⅔ cup milk
½ teaspoon salt	½ cup raisins
⅔ cup sweet butter	½ cup chopped nuts
½ cup brown sugar	2½ cups bran
½ cup honey	

Mix together the flour, baking powder, cinnamon and salt. Melt the butter and stir in the sugar and honey. Beat the eggs well, and add them to the butter mixture. Mix the soda and vanilla into the milk, then add the milk and butter mixtures alternately to the dry ingredients. When well mixed, add to the batter the raisins, nuts and bran, and mix in well. Drop by teaspoonfuls onto a well-greased baking sheet, an inch or more apart, and bake at 400° for about 10 minutes.

About 50 cookies

RECIPE #3

BROWNIES

These are the fudge type, very rich in chocolate.
rich by adding ½ teaspoon baking powder, an extra
egg, and ½ cup more flour, and reducing the cho-

1 cup butter	6 ounces (squares)
2 cups sugar	baking chocolate
3 eggs	1 cup wheat flour
1 teaspoon vanilla	½ teaspoon salt
	1 cup chopped nuts

Cream the sugar and half the butter. Beat the eggs
well, and mix them and the vanilla into the butter
mixture. Melt the rest of the butter with the
chocolate, cool and mix into the butter mixture.
Beat in the salt and flour until thoroughly mixed,
then stir in the nuts (if you like). Pour into a
well-greased and floured 9″ x 13″ baking pan and
bake at 350° for about 45 minutes, and cut into
squares or bars while still warm.

VARIATION: You can make these lighter and less

colate to 4 ounces.

RECIPE #4

CINNAMON COOKIES

¾ cup butter	*about 2 cups wheat*
1 cup brown sugar	*flour*
2 eggs	*cinnamon*

Cream the butter and sugar. Beat the eggs and mix into the butter mixture. Stir in enough flour to make a dough that can be gathered into a fairly stiff ball. Chill for at least an hour, roll out about ⅛-inch thick, cut into squares (or shapes, if you like) and sprinkle well with cinnamon. (If you brush the cookies with milk or melted butter first, the cinnamon will stick on better.) Bake on an ungreased baking sheet at 375° for about 10 minutes.

About 40 cookies

RECIPE #5

COCONUT JUMBLES

1 cup sweet butter	*5 eggs*
1½ cups powdered	*about 3 cups wheat*
sugar	*flour*
½ teaspoon salt	*2 cups grated coconut*

Cream the butter and sugar, and mix in the salt and well-beaten eggs. Mix in enough flour to make a fairly loose batter, then fold in the coconut. Drop from a spoon onto a well-greased and floured baking tin. Bake at 375° for 12 to 15 minutes.

About 60 2-inch cookies

RECIPE #6

DATE BARS

1 cup sugar
½ cup butter
2 eggs
1 cup wheat or rye
  flour

½ teaspoon baking
  powder
½ teaspoon salt
1 cup chopped dates
½ cup chopped nuts
  (optional)

Cream the sugar and butter until light and fluffy, then beat in the well-beaten eggs. Mix together the flour, baking powder and salt, and beat the dry ingredients into the liquid until thoroughly mixed. Stir in the dates and nuts, and pour the batter into a well-greased and floured 9″ square baking pan. Bake at 350° for about 20 minutes, and cut into squares or bars while still warm.

RECIPE #7

DESSERT BISCUITS

This is a basic drop-type sugar cookie that's quick and easy to make. Use any kind of whole-grain flour with any kind of flavoring you like, and call the cookies by any name.

½ cup sugar
½ cup butter
3 egg yolks

1½ cups flour
flavoring

Cream the butter and sugar, beat in the egg yolks, and beat in the flour and flavoring. Drop from a teaspoon onto a well-greased baking sheet. Bake at 375° for about 12 minutes.

SUGGESTIONS: Use wheat flour, honey instead of sugar, and ½ cup raisins or nuts. Use buckwheat flour, ¼ cup sherry, and 1 cup chopped dates or fruitcake mix. Use rolled oats, 1 cup raisins, and flavor with cinnamon, cloves, nutmeg, etc. Use rye flour, molasses instead of sugar, and 1 teaspoon ginger. Use half wheat flour and half cornmeal, add 1 teaspoon vanilla and 1 cup chocolate chips.

About 30 cookies

RECIPE #8

RICH GINGERBREAD NUTS

1 cup light molasses
½ cup melted sweet
 butter
1 cup raw sugar (or
 dark brown sugar)
½ teaspoon salt
1 tablespoon ground
 ginger
1½ teaspoons ground
 coriander

1 teaspoon caraway seed
1½ teaspoons grated
 orange rind
1 teaspoon grated
 lemon rind
1 egg
about 2 cups wheat
 flour (or 1 cup wheat
 and 1 cup rye)

Beat together the molasses and melted butter, and
beat in the sugar. Add the salt, spices, orange and
lemon rind, and beat thoroughly. Add the egg and
beat until well mixed. Add enough flour to make a
workable dough. Roll with your hands into 1-inch
nuts (if you chill the dough for a few hours, it's
easier to work). Bake on a greased baking sheet at
325° for 25 to 30 minutes.

About 50 nuts

RECIPE #9

HONEY GINGER NUTS

1 cup honey
1 cup sugar
½ cup melted butter
1 egg
2 cups wheat flour
¼ teaspoon salt

2 teaspoons baking
 powder
2 teaspoons ground
 ginger
1 cup chopped nuts

Mix together the honey, sugar and butter, and beat in the egg. Mix together the flour, salt, baking powder, and ginger, and beat the dry ingredients into the liquid until well mixed. Stir in the nuts and drop from a teaspoon onto a well-greased baking sheet. Bake at 350° for about 25 minutes.

About 40 cookies

RECIPE #10

GINGER SNAPS

1 cup butter
1 cup sugar
1 cup molasses
2 eggs
1 tablespoon vinegar
2 cups wheat flour

2 cups rye flour
2 teaspoons soda
1 tablespoon ginger
1 teaspoon cinnamon
½ teaspoon cloves

Cream the butter and sugar, beat in the molasses, then beat in the eggs and vinegar. Mix together the flours, soda and spices, and beat the dry ingredients into the liquid until well-mixed. Add a little flour if necessary to make a fairly workable dough. Shape into about ¾ inch balls and bake on a well-greased baking sheet at 325° for about 12 minutes.

About 140 small cookies

RECIPE #11

GRAHAM CRACKERS

It's fun to bake your own, but this recipe is simple enough for the children to help.

4 cups graham flour
1½ teaspoons baking powder
1 teaspoon salt

½ cup sweet butter or lard
about 1¼ cups milk

Mix together the flour, baking powder and salt, and rub in the shortening. Add enough milk to make a stiff dough. Knead for 10 minutes on a lightly floured board. Roll out very thin, cut into squares, and bake on an ungreased baking sheet at 350° for about 10 minutes.

About 70 3-inch crackers

RECIPE #12

HERMITS   *delicious*

1 C. SUGAR   ½ C. HONEY

1½ cups brown sugar
½ cup butter
1 egg
½ cup sour cream
2 cups wheat flour or cornmeal (or 1 cup of each)

1 teaspoon cinnamon
½ teaspoon cloves
½ teaspoon soda
½ cup raisins
½ cup nuts

Cream the sugar and butter, beat in the egg, then beat in the sour cream. Mix together the flour, spices and soda, and beat into the liquid. Stir in the raisins and nuts. Drop from a teaspoon onto a greased baking sheet and bake at 375° for about 15 minutes.

About 40 cookies

RECIPE #13

PLAIN HONEY COOKIES

6 tablespoons honey   ¼ teaspoon salt
6 tablespoons sweet   ¾ cup wheat flour
    butter   ¾ cup cornmeal

Melt the honey and butter together. Mix together
the flour, cornmeal and salt, pour the honey mixture on the dry ingredients and beat well. Knead
well until you have a workable dough, then roll out
very thin and cut into rounds. Bake on a greased
baking sheet at 300° for about 12 minutes.

About 30 cookies

RECIPE #14

HONEY SPICE COOKIES

2 eggs   ¼ teaspoon nutmeg
¾ cup sugar   ¼ teaspoon ginger
¾ cup honey   ½ teaspoon soda
½ teaspoon cinnamon   about 2 cups wheat
¼ teaspoon cloves   flour

Beat the eggs with the sugar until light and frothy
(but save about 1 tablespoon of egg white). Warm
the honey and beat it and the spices into the
liquid. Mix the soda into the flour and then beat
into the liquid. Add a little more flour if necessary
to make the dough firm enough to shape into a ball.
Chill the dough, in a covered bowl for 3 or 4 hours.
Knead it a little to soften it, roll it out about ¼

inch thick and cut it into shapes. Brush the tops of the cookies with egg white, and bake on a well-greased and floured baking sheet at 375° for about 10 minutes.

About 40 cookies

RECIPE #15

HONEY FRUIT NUGGETS

½ cup fruitcake mix (or about 3 tablespoons each chopped citron, candied orange peel, and candied lemon peel)
½ cup chopped blanched almonds
½ teaspoon grated lemon rind
1 tablespoon cinnamon
1 teaspoon cloves
1¼ cups powdered sugar
3 eggs
2 tablespoons orange juice
1 cup honey
1 tablespoon water
2½ cups wheat flour
1½ teaspoons soda

Mix together the fruitcake mix, almonds, lemon rind, spices and sugar. Beat the eggs well, with the orange juice and add to the first mixture. Boil the honey with the water, cool, and add to the first mixture. Combine the flour and soda and beat into the rest of the batter. Cover and let stand overnight (for 12 hours or more). Drop the batter from a teaspoon onto a greased baking sheet, 2 or 3 inches apart. Top each cookie with a blanched almond. Bake at 350° for 10 to 15 minutes.

About 80 cookies

RECIPE #16

LEMON CORNMEAL COOKIES

1½ cups cornmeal
½ cup wheat flour
½ cup butter
1 cup powdered sugar
2 eggs

1 tablespoon grated
   lemon rind
1½ teaspoons lemon
   juice

Mix together the flour and cornmeal, rub in the butter, and mix in the sugar. Beat the eggs well, and beat the lemon rind and juice into them, then add the liquid to the dry ingredients and beat well. Drop the batter from a spoon onto a well-greased baking sheet, about 2 inches apart. Bake at 350° for 15 to 20 minutes.

RECIPE #17

MOLASSES COOKIES

1 cup molasses
1 cup sugar
1 egg
¾ cup sweet butter
1 teaspoon salt
2 teaspoons cinnamon

1 teaspoon cloves
1 teaspoon ginger
1 tablespoon vinegar
2 cups cornmeal
about 1½ cups rye flour

Beat together the molasses, sugar and egg. Melt the butter, cool a little, and beat into the molasses mixture. Add the salt and spices and beat well. Then beat in the vinegar, the cornmeal, then enough rye flour to make a dough that can be gathered into a ball. Chill for 3 or 4 hours, roll out thin, and cut into shapes. Bake on an ungreased baking sheet at 350° for 10 or 15 minutes.

About 60 cookies

RECIPE #18

OATMEAL COOKIES

1 cup uncooked rolled
   oats
1 cup wheat flour
¾ cup brown sugar
1½ teaspoons baking
   powder
1½ teaspoons cinnamon

½ teaspoon salt
1 egg
½ cup milk
¼ cup melted butter
1 cup nuts and/or
   raisins (optional)

Mix together the oatmeal, flour, sugar, baking powder, cinnamon and salt. Beat the egg well, and mix it with the milk and butter. Beat the liquid into the dry ingredients until thoroughly mixed. Fold in the raisins and/or nuts, and drop from a teaspoon onto a greased baking sheet. Bake at 375° for 10 or 15 minutes.

About 40 cookies

RECIPE #19

OATMEAL WAFERS

3 eggs
2 cups sugar
2 tablespoons melted
   butter
1 teaspoon vanilla

1 teaspoon salt
1 cup shredded
   coconut
2 cups uncooked rolled
   oats

Beat the eggs well, then beat in the sugar gradually. Stir in the butter, vanilla and salt, then stir in the coconut and oatmeal. Drop from a teaspoon onto a well-greased, well-floured baking sheet. Bake at 350° for about 10 minutes.

35 to 40 cookies

RECIPE #20

PLAIN REFRIGERATOR COOKIES

This is a basic recipe that takes well to any kind of variation in flavoring or kind of flour.

1 cup sugar   *2 cups wheat flour*
½ cup sweet butter   *1 teaspoon salt*
1 egg   *2 teaspoons baking*
1 teaspoon vanilla   *powder*

Cream the sugar and butter, and add the well beaten egg and the vanilla. Mix together the flour, salt and baking powder, and gradually beat the dry ingredients into the liquid. Shape the dough into a long round loaf about 2 inches in diameter, wrap it well, and chill overnight. When you're ready to bake the cookies, slice the loaf into cookies about ⅛ inch thick (use a very sharp knife). Bake on an ungreased baking sheet at 375° for about 10 minutes.

VARIATIONS: 1. Substitute ½ cup honey or molasses for ½ cup of the sugar, to make a chewier cookie (you'll have to add a little extra flour so you can shape the dough into a loaf). 2. Use half wheat flour and half cornmeal, add 4 ounces (squares) of melted baking chocolate, 1 cup finely chopped pecans, and a little extra flour (this is very rich and chocolaty).

About 40 cookies

RECIPE #21

ROCK BISCUITS

This is a puffy, egg-rich cookie that keeps well. You can add any flavoring you like.

6 eggs
2 cups sugar
About 1½ cups wheat
  flour

raisins or nuts
  (optional)

Beat the eggs until very light, then beat in the sugar. Stir in the flour gradually and mix well (add just enough flour to make a light, non-runny dough). With a fork, put mounds of dough on a well-greased baking sheet, making the cookies as rough-looking as possible. Bake at 350° for about 25 minutes.

About 50 cookies

RECIPE #22

PLAIN RYE RINGS

1 cup butter
½ cup sugar

2½ to 3 cups rye flour

Cream the butter and sugar until light and fluffy. Mix in the flour thoroughly, and chill for about an hour. Roll out dough as thin as possible between two sheets of waxed paper. Prick the surface with a fork all over. Cut into rings (use a doughnut cutter, or make circles with a cookie cutter and cut out the centers with a thimble, bottle cap, etc.). Bake on a greased and floured baking sheet at 350° for 8 to 10 minutes.

About 30 cookies

RECIPE #23

CARAWAY RYE COOKIES

½ cup lard   1 teaspoon soda
½ cup butter   About 3 cups rye flour
1½ cups sugar   2 tablespoons caraway
1 cup sour milk   seed

Cream the lard, butter and sugar. Mix together the sour milk and soda. Mix together the flour and caraway seed. Add the liquid and the dry ingredients alternately to the butter mixture, and mix thoroughly. Use enough flour to make a dough that can be gathered into a ball. Chill for 3 or 4 hours, roll out very thin between waxed paper, and cut into shapes. Bake on a greased baking sheet at 400° for 5 to 8 minutes.

About 50 cookies

RECIPE #24

RYE-HONEY COOKIES

A hard, chewy, flat cookie.

2 cups honey   1½ teaspoons ground
About 2 cups rye flour   ginger

Heat the honey until it's liquid. Mix together the
flour and ginger, and warm in a skillet, being very
careful that the flour doesn't start to change color.
Beat the flour into the hot honey gradually, until
the dough is stiff enough to separate from the
spoon. Chill for 3 or 4 hours, roll as thin as possible
on a floured board, and cut into rounds. Bake on a
greased baking tin at 350° for 10 to 12 minutes.

About 100 cookies

RECIPE #25

WHEAT SHORTBREAD

1 cup sweet butter   About 3 cups wheat
½ cup powdered sugar   flour
¼ teaspoon almond
  extract (optional)

Cream the butter and sugar, beat in the almond
extract, and gradually beat in the flour. When the
dough is very smooth, divide it into three pieces.
Roll out each piece—on a greased baking sheet—
into a square about an inch thick, flute the edges by
pinching the dough all around, and bake at 350°
for about 25 minutes. Cut into squares or bars
while still warm.

RECIPE #26

HONEY SHORTBREAD

1 cup butter
½ cup sugar
2 tablespoons honey

About 2 cups wheat flour

Cream the butter and sugar and beat in the honey. Add the flour gradually and beat well. When smooth, press the dough into a greased shallow 8″ or 9″ square baking pan. Bake at 325° for about 25 minutes. Cut into squares or bars while still warm.

INDEX

135